Taming the Abrasive Manager

Taming the Abrasive Manager

How to End Unnecessary Roughness in the Workplace

Laura Crawshaw

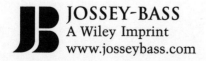

JOSSEY-BASS
A Wiley Imprint
www.josseybass.com

BICENTENNIAL
1807
WILEY
2007
BICENTENNIAL

Published by Jossey-Bass.
A Wiley Imprint
989 Market Street, San Francisco, CA 94103-1741   www.josseybass.com

Readers should be aware that Internet Web sites offered as citations and/or sources for further information may have changed or disappeared between the time this was written and when it is read.

Jossey-Bass books and products are available through most bookstores. To contact Jossey-Bass directly call our Customer Care Department within the U.S. at 800-956-7739, outside the U.S. at 317-572-3986, or fax 317-572-4002.

Jossey-Bass also publishes its books in a variety of electronic formats. Some content that appears in print may not be available in electronic books.

Library of Congress Cataloging-in-Publication Data

Crawshaw, Laura, 1953–
    Taming the abrasive manager : how to end unnecessary roughness in the workplace / Laura Crawshaw.
        p. cm.
    Includes bibliographical references and index.
    ISBN 978-0-7879-8837-1 (cloth)
    1. Managing your boss.   2. Organizational behaviour.   3. Interpersonal relation.   I. Title
    HF5548.83.C73 2007
    650.1'3—dc22

                                                            2007011826

Printed in the United States of America
FIRST EDITION

HB Printing   10 9 8 7 6 5 4 3 2 1

The Jossey-Bass

Business & Management Series

Contents

[T]he fear ... struck into their hearts was too deep to be dislodged. ... [T]here were those ... who understood this. They could see into the creature's soul and soothe the wounds they found there. ... For secrets uttered softly into ... troubled ears, these ... were known as Whisperers.

−Nicholas Evans, The Horse Whisperer

The Author

Laura Crawshaw received her MSW degree in clinical social work from the Smith College School for Social Work and conducted postgraduate studies at the Seattle Institute for Psychoanalysis and Harvard Community Health Plan. She completed both MA and PhD degrees in human and organizational systems at Fielding Graduate University. Laura founded the Executive Insight Development Group in 1994, an international firm offering psychodynamically based coaching services for abrasive leaders and dysfunctional teams; Executive Insight has served an international clientele of corporations, including over forty Fortune 500 companies. With over thirty years' experience as a psychotherapist, corporate officer, and executive coach, Laura now focuses her research and practice on the reduction of workplace suffering. She is a member of the International Society for the Psychoanalytic Study of Organizations, the American Psychological Association, and the International Coach Federation. Laura particularly enjoys the company of human and nonhuman members of the animal kingdom. She can be contacted at *www.executiveinsight.com.*

This book is dedicated to my wonderful parents, without whose love, humor, and insight I would not be who and where I am today; to two great bosses, Darryl Logan and Jay Youell; and to my coaching clients, who had the courage to change.

I also wish to thank my dear friends who supported me on this journey, and those members of the animal kingdom who allowed me to share in their worlds, especially members of the species Ursus arctos horribilis and Canis lupus familiarus puggus.

Finally, thanks to my editor and expert author whisperer, Neal Maillet, who knew exactly how to tame my anxieties.

Introduction

I'm too impatient to read book introductions—why waste time reading about what I'm about to read? Why not just cut to the chase and get to the meat of the matter? I'm sure I've missed some important information in these books because of my carnivorous reading style, but because I can't stand to wade through lengthy introductions, I'm going to make this short.

You're reading this book because you

- *Manage* someone who is abrasive
- Work *with* someone who is abrasive
- Work *for* someone who is abrasive

In other words, you are the superior, peer, or subordinate of an abrasive manager. You are tired, frustrated, and distressed. You have either tried everything you can think of to tame the abrasive manager's aggressive behavior, to no avail, or you are too afraid to try anything, for fear of what could happen. This book is written for you.

You already know a few things about abrasive managers (or *abrasive bosses*, as I refer to them in this book) from your own experience. You know that they're usually blind to their destructive impact on coworkers ("they just don't get it—they just don't see"), and if they do see, they don't seem to care.

To have any hope of taming an abrasive boss, you need to know *why* these bosses do what they do and what you can (and can't) do about it. With the help of this book, which is based on my years of research with abrasive bosses and their coworkers, you'll learn how to make them *see* the damage they inflict and how to make them *care* enough to rein in their aggressive behavior. Now, let's cut to the chase. . .

Taming the Abrasive Manager

1

Abrasive Bosses and the Working Wounded

Abrasive bosses rub their coworkers the wrong way. Their words and actions create interpersonal friction that grates on subordinates, peers, and superiors, grinding away at trust and motivation. Abrasive bosses can inflict deep wounds and intense suffering in employees. The pain of working with an abrasive boss is often felt by the company as well, eroding effectiveness and paralyzing productivity. Few of us have escaped the pain of working under, over, or with an abrasive boss, and far too many of us have unwillingly entered the ranks of what I have come to call the *working wounded.*

I coach abrasive bosses of all kinds: executives, managers, supervisors, and professionals (physicians, attorneys, others) whose disruptive behaviors cause profound emotional distress in the people they work with. Over the past two decades I have had the opportunity to closely observe how and why these abrasive bosses rub coworkers the wrong way. I've also examined the individual and organizational wounds they inflict, listening to the pain experienced by their subordinates, peers, and superiors and, believe it or not, by the abrasive bosses themselves. I've written this book to share my observations and offer my insights on why abrasive bosses resort to aggression, why individuals and organizations fail to intervene effectively, and, most important, what you can (and can't) do about it. In medicine, *abrasion* refers to the physical trauma sustained when exposed skin rubs against a rough surface. In this book, *workplace abrasion* refers to the psychological trauma sustained when employees are exposed to the unnecessary roughness of an abrasive boss. Both scenarios produce suffering.

It Only Hurts When I Work

Suffering is a term rarely applied in the workplace. It's one of those emotionally loaded (also referred to as *touchy-feely*) words that seem out of place at work. Aren't we supposed to leave our emotions at the door so we can get on with business? Workplace *suffering*? Employers don't want to hear about it because they don't want to be perceived as perpetrators of suffering—they're there to get the job done, and social services aren't part of that picture. Second, it's a given that we all were meant to suffer at work—right? Showing up day after day to plug away at tasks we don't necessarily enjoy with people we don't necessarily like is a pain, a pain that most of us can't afford to avoid. What lottery winner doesn't jubilantly declare that his or her first act will be to quit work? Unless we are lucky enough to love what we do and the people we do it with, we endure the assorted discomforts of work to pay the bills and keep the wolves from the door. So since when *isn't* work supposed to be painful?

Work can be painful for other reasons, including the actual nature of the work. Early man learned early on that woolly mammoth hunts were no picnic if you were the one who ended up trampled or impaled. And it seems pretty obvious that pyramid building was no easy task for your average Aztec or Egyptian laborer. As a kid I remember teachers warning us of the physical and mental suffering we would endure digging ditches or screwing caps on toothpaste tubes if we failed to hit the books. It's not only the nature of the work that can be unpleasant or uninteresting, causing physical or emotional suffering—work can also hurt because of the circumstances surrounding our jobs: weak wages, bleak benefits, bad schedules, or looming layoffs. In short, work can be a pain.

But the pain of work itself is not the pain I'm addressing in this book. Nor am I talking about the pain caused by bosses who cut programs, pay, or people based on business need. I'm talking about the pain suffered from direct contact with an abrasive boss; the emotional wounds sustained from *direct interpersonal aggression* experienced in day-to-day interactions with abrasive bosses. And the suffering isn't limited to abrasive bosses' subordinates: all of their coworkers—subordinates, peers, and superiors alike—can be rubbed raw by the grinding force of disrespectful treatment:

"He's always talking down to people, interrogating them—'*Why didn't you do this? Why didn't you do that?*'—he makes people feel like idiots."

"Everyone feels helpless, hopeless, out of control."

"She does what's best for her—she doesn't stand up for us, ever. If she's questioned by management, she comes back and attacks without exploring the issue."

"It leaves us feeling so unimportant—like we're not worth anything."

"We're all afraid of him; he walks around, sees something that sets him off and starts yelling. It gets so tense—to the point where no one wants to even talk. It's getting harder to come to work."

"The best days at work are the days she isn't here—that's when we can breathe."

"Working here reminds me of the time I was in an abusive relationship. I find myself thinking 'What's wrong with me? What am I doing wrong? What can I do differently?' I've never had that experience in my work life until this new manager showed up."

"I used to enjoy coming to work, but since she's been here, all I can think about is finding a way to get out."

"He's not a team player. It's never 'we'; it's always '*I want*,' '*I said.*'"

"When he shows up, we shut up. We don't tell him any more than we have to because you don't want to bring up anything that will provoke him."

"Her behavior shouldn't be tolerated. We shouldn't have to constantly walk on eggshells."

"People get a sick stomach when he walks through the department."

"It all boils down to respect—when you feel your efforts are appreciated, when you see some interest in what you're doing, that's respect. I can't deal with the contempt, the ugly mood swings, his refusal to treat his team with respect."

To Kick or Not to Kick

The suffering caused by abrasive bosses is not only injurious, it's also inefficient. Typically, at the outset of coaching, my abrasive clients will argue this point, insisting that unless they "kick ass," the work won't get done. In his landmark article "One More Time: How Do You Motivate Employees?" renowned management researcher Frederick Herzberg (1968) termed this the KITA (kick-in-the-you-know-what) approach to management. However, the KITA approach presents certain drawbacks. Herzberg listed the limitations of physically kicking one's coworkers:

(1) it is inelegant; (2) it contradicts the precious image of benevolence that most organizations cherish; and (3) since it is a physical attack, it directly stimulates the autonomic nervous system, and this often results in negative feedback—the employee may just kick you in return [p. 54].

Physical KITA and psychological KITA appear to be equally ineffective in building internal motivation:

Why is KITA not motivation? If I kick my dog (from the front or the back), he will move. And when I want him to move again, what must I do? I must kick him again. . . . But it is only when one has a generator of one's own that we can talk about motivation. One then needs no outside stimulation. One *wants* to do it [p. 55].

Abrasive bosses manage for movement rather than motivation. They are blind to the fact that external intimidation does nothing to build internal motivation; they are blind to the reality that employees respond more positively to carrots than sticks. Abrasive bosses flog their coworkers into movement, whereas insightful (or what I will term *adequate*) bosses use positive strategies to make their employees *want* to move. They rely on the carrots of positive reward, unwilling to resort to psychological horsewhippings. And in the rare instances where employees refuse to move at the required pace, adequate bosses understand that beating a nearly dead horse is not only cruel—it's also inefficient. Instead, they cut the employee from the herd through the civilized processes of formal termination. Abrasive bosses approach motivation very differently, and in the next chapters we'll be looking at how, when, and why abrasive bosses kick their coworkers.

Speaking of motivation, you may be wondering what motivates me to coach abrasive bosses. I'm going to confess something that I never reveal to prospective corporate clients. Ready? My *mission is to reduce suffering in the workplace*. I dare not speak of this mission when I talk with companies struggling with an abrasive boss—it absolutely reeks of touchy-feely. I don't want these hard-nosed business folks to suspect that they're hiring a bleeding-heart social worker, do I? Social service types are highly suspect in the work world; we're perceived as do-gooders intent on disrupting hard business objectives with the "soft" stuff of putting individual needs over organizational objectives. Woody Allen once described a nightmare in which he was pursued by a monster with the body of a crab and the head of a social worker. My body is quite human, but I spare my corporate clients the prospect of any such do-gooder nightmares by concealing my mission and instead making the case for coaching in a language they understand: facts and numbers.

The Costs of Abrasion

Let's ignore the soft stuff for a moment and take a hard look at the scope and costs of organizational disruption caused by abrasive bosses. For those of you who need numbers, I offer these: A Gallup study of 2 million workers at 700 companies found that poor supervisory behavior was the main reason that employees quit or were less productive (Work & Family Connection, 2005). A study of superior-to-subordinate aggression in the United Kingdom concluded that close to 2.5 million UK employees considered themselves to have been victims of managerial aggression in the previous six months (Hoel & Cooper, 2000). Research conducted by the Center for Creative Leadership (Lombardo & McCall, 1984) reported that 74 percent of successful executives in three Fortune 100 corporations said they had had at least one intolerable boss, and another study (Spherion Corporation, 1999) showed that employees are four times more likely to leave bosses who are not considered "nice" (another word rarely used in a business context). Attrition of valued employees is just one of the prices paid. In the past decade researchers have explored other costs incurred by abrasive bosses: decreased morale and motivation resulting in absenteeism and lowered productivity (McCarthy, Sheehan, & Kearns, 1995), higher incidence of stress-related illnesses (Quine, 1999) and substance abuse (Richman, Rospenda, Flaherty, & Freels, 2001), increased number of legal actions alleging a hostile environment or discriminatory behavior (Leymann, 1990), and retaliatory responses, including sabotage (Laabs, 1999) and homicide (McLaughlin, 2000; Rayner, 1997).

Had enough? Do I really need to swamp you with more statistics to convince you that abrasive bosses take a serious toll on both employee and employer? Employers not only lose employees; they lose hundreds of thousands of hours of productivity while workers focus on the pain of abrasion instead of the tasks at hand. Think for a moment—how many hours have you seen coworkers

spend around the coffee machine or behind closed doors process-
ing the latest painful run-in with an abrasive boss? I have yet
to see any formal research on the number of hours management
(including human resource staff) devotes to abrasive boss-related
issues, but those I have spoken with resent the "waste" (their
word) of time that could be better spent on other concerns. I
could devote many more pages to documenting the costs incurred
by abrasive bosses, but the fact that you are reading this book
suggests that you don't need to be convinced—I suspect you've
already paid a price.

A Bleeding Heart Is Born

Enough of the hard stuff—let's get back to my soft-hearted goal of
reducing workplace suffering caused by abrasive bosses. As I read
this, I realize that I may be giving the mistaken impression that I
aspire to be the Mother Theresa of executive coaching, which is
not the case. I don't do what I do because I am divinely inspired
or in the least bit noble. *It's my parents' fault—I blame them.*

Too often parents are blamed for everything that we don't
like about ourselves, but I am pleased to blame my parents for
teaching me that the most important use of one's life lies in
helping others. I learned about suffering from my psychiatrist
father and hospital volunteer mother—not at their hands but
through their hearts and eyes. I was blessed with a safe, loving
home and only encountered suffering as I ventured out into the
wider world.

My earliest lessons of suffering were taught by animals. When
I was very little, my mother took me to a Tarzan movie where a
mortally wounded elephant slowly found its way to the elephant
graveyard to die. The pain and sadness that reverberated through
me was excruciating—I was distraught. I remember my mother's
efforts to comfort her sobbing child, wiping my tears away,
assuring me that the elephant was just acting and that it had

been given a special treat of canned dog food once it finished "playing pretend."

A later experience of intense suffering also involved animals. I must have been six or seven years old, and my father, founder of a local children's mental health clinic, hosted a charity carnival to raise funds for the clinic. It was a typical rainy day in Oregon, and the carnival had a kiddy ride with ponies tied to a rotating frame. I remember the wet, downcast ponies, trudging around and around in a circle of mud, and to this day the memory cuts through me like a knife. I believed they wanted to be free (or at least loved) instead of being chained to a muddy merry-go-round for human entertainment. I felt terribly sad, knowing that I could do nothing to relieve their suffering. I believe this childhood experience of helplessness in the face of suffering formed the foundation for my adult wish to reduce suffering by eventually becoming a psychotherapist and, later, an executive coach.

Intent on becoming a psychiatrist, I embarked on a premed track in college. As I wrestled with my courses, it gradually dawned on me that I was never going to succeed as a physician because, frankly, I didn't have the patience or interest to memorize every bone, sinew, and organ of the human anatomy. I figured it would be pretty unethical to even consider the practice of medicine if I wasn't willing to memorize everything ("*I'm sorry sir, but I'm hesitant to remove your appendix because I never bothered to learn what it's connected to*"). I wanted to study psyche, not physique, and was fortunate enough to discover that I could become a psychotherapist without pursuing a medical degree. So I abandoned my medical pretensions and instead pursued a degree in clinical (or what was then called psychiatric) social work.

Working Wounded on the Last Frontier

Degree in hand, I moved to Seattle with the plan of paying my dues by working in respected settings and eventually opening a private practice to treat emotionally disturbed children. To that end I enrolled in the Child Therapy Certificate Program of the Seattle Institute for Psychoanalysis, where I was privileged to be clinically supervised by Edith Buxbaum, a student of Anna Freud. After two years of seeing patients in a community mental health clinic and working nights as an emergency room social worker in a major trauma center, I experienced two revelations. First, I realized that if I were to become a private practitioner, I would have to sit in a room, *inside, all day, every day*. Whoa— this heart not only bled, it wandered as well. The prospect of being cooped up in the same clinical stall every day made me want to hightail it out of there. Second, it became clear to me that Seattle was overrun with psychotherapists—I'd have to wait until a fair number of them dropped dead before I could have any hope of opening a viable practice. I'm not the deathwatch type, and beyond this, I was (and still am) a total tourist—I lusted to explore the wider world beyond the four walls of a clinical office. So I heeded the call of the wild, purchased a ferry ticket north to Alaska, and bolted. There were jobs aplenty in the Last Frontier, and who knew what other experiences awaited?

Within a week of my arrival, I was hired as the first full-time clinician in the first stand-alone employee assistance program (EAP) in the state, embarking on the greatest adventures any tenderfoot clinician could hope for. EAPs provide confidential counseling services to employees and eligible family members experiencing problems in their personal or work lives. Our initially tiny company eventually provided counseling to Alaskan employees (and family members) of over 600 corporations throughout the state. I was trucked up and down the Alaska pipeline in −70°F (−56°C) temperatures to explain the benefits of EAP counseling to pump station employees and helicoptered out to Bering Sea drill rigs to deliver the same message to exhausted roustabouts. Back at the office igloo I counseled employees on the problems they experienced at work and home, learning that shooting a spouse's sled dogs was a reliable indicator of marital distress in Alaska. Another indicator of marital peril lay in the discovery by one newlywed that her gun-loving, hard-drinking husband's past two wives were buried on her new love's wilderness homestead. I referred unwilling addicted air traffic controllers into substance abuse treatment and helped wildlife biologists cope with their fears of flying. It was truly the Last Frontier—right down to the guns.

Armed Defense

The *guns?* I encountered the guns in the course of my counseling work. The typical scenario consisted of a call from an employee for a same-day appointment because he (they were always men) "needed to talk to someone right away." We took these quiet, urgent calls seriously, reshuffling our schedules for such sudden requests. I would find myself seated across from the client, who was usually withdrawn and obviously embarrassed to be sitting in a counselor's office. My questions of "How can I help you? Could you tell me what's going on?" would elicit a halting story of suffering. The suffering was inflicted by the employee's boss, whose behavior could take many forms, such as tyrannical control or public humiliation of the employee. The variations never failed to amaze me, but the common theme was of abrasive behavior that had pushed the employee to the point of . . . what? To find the answer, I uttered the psychotherapist's classic question:

> *Counselor:* And how does this make you feel?
> *Employee:* Like getting back at him.
> *Counselor:* Have you thought of how you would do that?
> *Employee:* Yeah. [*An embarrassed silence.*] With a gun.
> *Counselor:* Do you have a gun?
> *Employee:* Uh . . . yeah . . . out in my truck. That's why I
> called you.

The same pain that cut through me as a child when confronted with suffering now sliced through my adult soul. This man was suffering—tormented by his impulses to silence his tormentor, shamed by his loss of control, and humiliated by his need to seek external restraint for his retaliatory impulses. He had reached the point where he saw his gun as his only remaining defense against his boss's aggression. He was one of many, and as the arsenal in our office safe increased, I wondered how this could be happening. Having experienced good parents and good bosses, I was mystified—why would bosses brutalize their employees, and how could companies tolerate this infliction of suffering? What were the dynamics of aggression and defense that created such profound anguish? These questions set this boss whisperer on a journey to understand these unmanageable managers and learn how to tame their abrasive aggression.

2

Boss Whispering

I have a confession to make: I don't call myself a boss whisperer in real life. I refer to myself as an executive coach, the standard term applied to coaches who work with businesspeople. I have mixed feelings about the executive coach label because it suggests that I restrict my coaching to the upper echelons of bossdom, otherwise known as the *C-level*: CEO, COO, CIO, CFO, and assorted other chiefs. I am distinctly uncomfortable with such an elitist conceptualization of coaching and have to restrain my potentially abrasive comments when other coaches boast that they work exclusively with top executives, as if this were some sort of badge of honor. I'm not terribly impressed with physicians who take pride in treating only the wealthy or powerful—it doesn't make them better doctors. Bosses at every level struggle with management challenges, and to limit their access to coaching because of the outrageous fees charged by many of these C-level coaches is, I believe, unethical. Tirade over.

Back to my confession about the boss whisperer title: when I was a doctoral student I couldn't resist buying a book whose title promised that a dissertation could be written in *only fifteen minutes a day*. What a promise! What a title! What a gimmick! Not far into the first chapter the author confessed that the probability of completing one's dissertation in one's lifetime by writing for only fifteen minutes a day was pretty low. She was right—I upped my minutes, finished my dissertation, and to this day admire her ability to come up with a catchy title and deliver some very helpful wisdom. I trust you'll excuse this so-called boss whisperer from using similar tactics so long as I pitch forth with some helpful horse (or should I say *boss*) sense.

Boss Whispering

Even though I don't initially refer to my work as boss whispering, the term roughly describes what I do. Much like the horse whisperer who calms unmanageable horses, I work to calm the fears that drive abrasive bosses to trample on others' emotions. I became a boss whisperer the same way that horse whisperers start, by carefully observing horses (or in my case, bosses) and trying to understand why they behave as they do. This requires trying to get into their heads and see the world through their eyes. This process of observing behavior in order to decipher its meaning is actually the process of empathy. Empathy doesn't mean *feeling for* (sympathy)—it means *feeling into*, or *feeling with*, as in putting one's self into the shoes (or hooves) of other beings to better understand the feelings that motivate their problematic behaviors. Using empathy, the whisperer gains insight into the abrasive behaviors and translates this insight into methods specifically designed to calm the horse (or boss) and eliminate the maladaptive behavior without the use of force or intimidation.

Calm the fears that drive abrasive bosses? Because of their intimidating, aggressive styles, it can be a stretch to believe that these fear-inspiring individuals *are themselves driven by fear*. I'll discuss this concept in greater detail in Chapter Four, but for now I want to emphasize that emotions *drive*, or *move*, behavior: the word *emotion* is derived from the Latin *emovere* ("to move out"). To understand behavior, one must seek to understand the underlying emotions that move (motivate) the behavior. I call this *reading* emotions—putting yourself in another's shoes (in other words, using empathy) to decipher the fears motivating problematic behavior. Horse whisperers spend a lot of time hanging around the ol' corral, observing what motivates horses to do what they do. As a subordinate, peer, executive, and boss whisperer, I've spent a lot of time in corporate corrals observing boss behavior. But my training in whispering started long before those years spent with bosses—I'd been reading emotions since I was knee-high to a psychiatrist.

My Apprenticeship in Emotional Literacy

Remember that my earliest lessons in suffering were taught by animals. However, my earliest lessons in reading emotions were imparted by humans and, more specifically, by my father. This should come as no surprise: if you're the child of an auto mechanic, chances are pretty good that you're going to learn more than the other kids on your block about how car engines work. Born to a psychoanalytically oriented psychiatrist, I grew up hearing a lot about people's psychological workings, otherwise known as *psychodynamics*. My dad didn't use that term with me—he just got me thinking about why people do what they do. For example: I was probably nine years old, sitting in a car with my dad at a stoplight, observing a disheveled man walking with a strange gait, shouting and waving his hands. "See that man over there?" my father asked. "He's probably schizophrenic." I somehow knew that schizophrenia meant mental illness, but I still questioned, "Couldn't it be that he just walks funny?" I don't remember my father's exact response, but in that early interchange I was being taught that behavior has meaning and that with psychological insight one can read the underlying meanings (motivations) of behavior. This man's behaviors were the external expressions of his internal struggle with psychosis.

These tutorials continued throughout my childhood. I have another memory of our family attending a banquet held for one of my father's colleagues. When we got home, my father commented that the man was depressed. *How could he possibly know that?* The man had made no mention of depressing events or depressed feelings. When I challenged my father, he responded with a description of what I would later learn to be vegetative symptoms of depression: "Well, he's normally talkative, but he said very little, never smiled, and hardly ate." My father was able to observe and interpret this constellation of behaviors (withdrawal, flat affect, disturbed appetite) as probable indicators of depression. What an education! I was learning by observing my father's exercise of psychological insight: the practice of *reading emotions to understand behavior*. Over time I gradually learned to observe behavior and do my best to accurately interpret its significance.

My education wasn't always fun. Psychiatrists read behavior, and let me tell you, it can be pretty irritating when you're the book they're reading. I remember telephoning my parents during my freshman year at college to nervously declare that I would not be coming home for Christmas vacation, instead planning to go on a car trip with my newfound friends. I remember my father pausing and then announcing, "What you really mean is that you wish to separate and individuate from your parents." I will be eternally grateful for my mother's retort: "Oh, for God's sake, Ralph. What she really means is that she just wants to be with her friends instead of her boring parents!" To this day I bridle whenever I hear the phrase, "What you *really* mean is . . . ," but that's what reading emotion is all about: deciphering the meaning behind our actions. (By the way, both parents were correct in their interpretations.)

My Education Continues

In the last chapter I shared my first encounters with the working wounded as an employee assistance counselor in Alaska. After ten years in that role I was recruited to go Outside (Alaskan slang for the Lower 48) to embark on my next career incarnation: executive in a global managed health care corporation. I rubbed shoulders with a few abrasive bosses (luckily, none of them mine) during those years, without incident—they were focused on others. I eventually left the corporate racetrack to hang out my shingle as a management consultant—I was on the trail to becoming a boss whisperer.

Over and over again I would be called in by a company to help with a "communication problem" (management's diagnosis). The typical scenario was of a boss in conflict with his or her subordinates, peers, or superiors. I'd interview the parties on both sides of the conflict, and on closer examination it would become obvious that one party (composed of the coworkers) was behaving reasonably and the other (namely, the boss) wasn't. More often than not it wasn't a simple case of differing ideas or objectives. Instead I would discover a chronic pattern of abrasive behavior on the boss's part that had strained working relationships to the breaking point. Coworkers were well into the defensive modes of fight or flight. They were either fighting the boss through active or passive resistance ("If he thinks I'm going to lift a finger for him after the way he treated me, he's got a big surprise coming") or fleeing through withdrawal ("I can't deal with her anymore—I avoid her at all costs"). I was puzzled. Why were these apparently intelligent bosses riding roughshod over their seemingly rational, dedicated coworkers?

Boss whisperers have a great advantage over horse whisperers in that bosses talk and horses don't. I wanted to understand what I was seeing, so I started talking to these bosses, carefully phrasing my questions so as not to provoke defensiveness. We psychotherapists are pretty good at concocting gentle questions that explore emotion and behavior—you've heard them before: "And how did that make you feel?" or "And why do you think you reacted that way?" By listening very carefully to put myself in their shoes, I was gradually able to see the world through their eyes and gain insight into the emotions that drove their abrasive behavior. I learned a lot, but before I put what I was learning into practice I wanted to compare my findings with others who had studied abrasive bosses.

My research began at the local bookstore, where I had no trouble finding a shelf loaded with books on abrasive bosses. These books bore remarkably similar characteristics, beginning with their melodramatic titles: *Jerks at Work* (Lloyd, 1999), *The Bully at Work* (Namie & Namie, 2003), *Corporate Hyenas at Work* (Marais & Herman, 1997), *Crazy Bosses* (Bing, 1992), *Snakes in Suits* (Babiak & Hare, 2006), and *Brutal Bosses and Their Prey* (Hornstein, 1996), to name a few. Talk about catchy titles! Authors referred variously to their books as *combat guides, survival guides, bullybusting strategies,* or *tyrant-toppling techniques*. The books typically consisted of an overview of the problem, followed by the author's commanding and colorful classification of boss types ranging from A(ssholes) to Z(ombies). Some examples: *Certified Asshole* (Sutton, 2007); *Bully, Paranoid, Narcissist, Bureaucrazy, Disaster Hunter* (Bing, 1992); *Executioner, Dehumanizer, Blamer, Rationalizer, Conqueror, Manipulator* (Hornstein, 1996); *Self-Involved Toxic Executive, Toxic Disorganizer, Valueless Toxic Executive* (Reed, 1993); *Constant Critic, Two-Headed Snake, Screaming Mimi* (Namie & Namie, 2003); *Angry Screamer, Saccharine Snake, Space Case, Invalidator, Cold Shoulder* (Felder, 1993); and *Casanova, Explosive, Gangster, Spineless Sensation, Turncoat, Backstabber, Accuser,* and *Zombie* (Di Genio, 2002). Even the authors of one of the earliest serious research efforts into intolerable bosses (their term), Michael Lombardo and Morgan McCall (1984), couldn't resist the seemingly irresistible lure of the lurid label, referring to these bosses as *Snakes in the Grass, Attilas, Heel Grinders, Egotists, Dodgers, Business Incompetents, Detail Drones,* and *Slobs*.

I was struck by this sensationalistic and frankly unprofessional approach to abrasive bosses. If I were to peruse the section devoted to child abuse in that same bookstore, would I find books titled *Evil Parents and Their Prey* or *Psychoparent-Busting Strategies*, complete with categories classifying parents as *Baby Bashers, Kiddy Kickers,* or *Toxic Tot-Tormentors*? The answer is no, because in today's society, child, spouse, and elder abuse are treated as serious issues deserving of serious attention. Demonizing people who inflict pain on others is understandable but irresponsible, and more important, it's unhelpful. I continually struggle to understand why we don't we take employee abuse as seriously as we do these other types of harm. We have a choice: we can view abrasive bosses as evil demons who cannot change (thereby keeping our distance), or we can seek to understand the phenomenon through serious research. I decided to pursue the latter option and devoted my doctoral work to developing a deeper understanding of the abrasive bosses that filled my coaching practice.

Disappointed and disgusted by most of what I'd discovered in my bookstore ramblings, I embarked on a review of the scholarly literature on abuse in the workplace, also termed *workplace bullying*. I had high hopes of learning about abrasive bosses but found that the research focused almost exclusively on the impact of workplace abuse on employees. I found numerous studies that explored the types of this abuse and its effects on employees, but I couldn't find any systematic studies conducted with the abrasive bosses themselves. Finally, I came upon an article that explained this gap, a gap termed the *black hole* of workplace abuse by researchers Rayner and Cooper (2003):

> Gathering data about black holes is difficult because we cannot see them. The gravity pull of the black hole is so strong that light, even at its great speed, cannot escape. We know black holes exist only because of celestial bodies around them, which, for example, change course or behave 'oddly', sometimes being 'eaten' by the crushing effect of the gravity pulls from the black hole.... For those who study negative behavior at work, 'the bully' is the parallel of black holes—almost invisible to us. We gain all our data regarding bullies from other people and events that happen around them.... Finding and studying the bully is like trying to study black holes—we are often chasing scattered debris of complex data and shadows of the past [p. 47].

Reading this, I was struck by a BFO—a blinding flash of the obvious. There was a reason that I couldn't find any studies of abrasive bosses: *there weren't any*. Researchers hadn't figured out a way to find them—companies certainly would be reluctant to admit that they had such individuals in their employ, and attempts to recruit participants through advertising wouldn't work either because most abrasive bosses don't see themselves as abrasive. Stumbling upon this black hole, I realized that researchers hadn't interviewed abrasive bosses. They hadn't been able to talk with them and learn why they kicked their coworkers. And then I had another blinding flash: *I'd been talking to abrasive bosses for years*—this boss whisperer had been getting data *straight from the horses' mouths*. My conversations weren't limited to those who'd been trampled by abrasive bosses—I'd spent thousands of hours talking with the tramplers as well. I realized I had collected valuable data over the years, data that became the foundation of my research on why abrasive bosses behave as they do and what can be done to help them change. I'm writing this book to share the insights I've developed from my research to help you tame the abrasive boss you manage, are managed by, or work with. But these insights aren't based only on research—they're also based on my observations of what does and doesn't work when intervening with these individuals. Over the years I've observed managers, subordinates, and peers test a wide variety of strategies to rein in an abrasive boss; some of them effective, others futile.

My guess is that you'd like me to cut to the chase and cough up the effective strategies. I could do that, *but they won't work if you don't know what you're dealing with*. No horse whisperer worth his or her salt would walk into a corral to tame a horse without a basic understanding of horse behavior—they need horse sense. The same holds true for taming abrasive bosses. Trust me, you don't want to enter the corporate corral without insight into their abrasive behavior. The next chapters will provide you with exactly that: *boss sense*. You'll learn who these abrasive bosses are, what they do, why they do it, why they don't see what they do, why they don't seem to care, what you can (and can't) do about it, and the risks involved. But before we get to that, there's something I've got to do. I've criticized other authors for their sensationalistic classifications of abrasive boss types, but it turns out I'm no different—even I can't resist the lure of labeling. Some people *gotta dance*, and I *gotta categorize!*

Actually, I am different, because my labels don't resemble the names of comic book villains—no *Satanic Supervisors* or *Maniac Managers* here. Instead, my labels describe behavioral styles without demonizing or denigrating. I chose the *abrasive boss* label because I believe it is descriptive without being disrespectful. You've probably noticed that I don't refer to abrasive bosses as "bullies." I dislike that label, for two reasons. First, I believe that calling someone a bully implies that these individuals *want* to hurt others, that they intentionally set out to do harm. I found the opposite case. I discovered that abrasive bosses don't intend to harm—their intent is to motivate. And if they do cause harm, more often than not they're blind to the fact that they've wounded others.

There's a second reason why I don't refer to abrasive bosses as bullies. I think it's unprofessional. When I reviewed the popular literature on abrasive bosses, I couldn't get over the fact that the so-called expert authors of these bully-battling books behaved like bullies themselves, indulging in derogatory, disrespectful descriptors of abrasive bosses. As I've noted, this phenomenon is peculiar to workplace abuse; researchers don't label those who engage in domestic abuse "bitch" or "bastard," so why do so-called "expert" authors feel free to use the bully label in reference to workplace abuse?

I suspect we treat abrasive bosses in this manner because we find it difficult to empathize with them. With child abusers we can put ourselves in their shoes to understand the intense psychological stressors that can drive parents to vent their distress on children. But it's much harder to step into the shoes of an abrasive boss. Empathy, *schmempathy*—aren't bosses supposed to have their psychological acts together? Aren't they grown adults, capable of managing people, projects, and their own psyches? Well, I hate to break it to you, but bosses are human, just like us. And just like abusive parents, some bosses lack the ability to manage their psychological stressors and end up venting their distress on those around them. As long as we demonize abrasive bosses, we can hold ourselves apart and avoid the challenging work of learning why they do what they do, and what we can do about it.

Definitions and Categories

Here's a list of definitions for terms that I will be using throughout the book. These may differ from how you've used these terms in the past, so please read carefully:

Boss: any individual charged with managerial authority, from CEO to mailroom supervisor. This authority may be formal (the individual has defined reporting relationships with others) or informal (the individual is empowered to exert influence over others without formally defined relationships: for example, a physician may direct nursing staff even though they do not formally report to the physician).

Manager: a boss's immediate superior; the abrasive boss's boss.

Management: collectively, the individuals who hold positions that are higher than the abrasive boss's position or who are authorized to exert influence over abrasive bosses (such as human resource or legal staff).

Peers: individuals who hold positions roughly equivalent in status to the abrasive boss's.

Subordinates: individuals who report directly to the abrasive boss.

Coworkers: all employees at any level who have contact with the abrasive boss; anyone working in the same organization.

Now, on to my boss categories. I've found these categories useful in my work with abrasive bosses; I have yet to encounter a boss who didn't fall into one of them. Please also note that I classify bosses according to their interpersonal conduct rather than their work performance. *Conduct* refers to *interpersonal competence*: the degree to which one interacts effectively with coworkers. *Performance*, in contrast, refers to *technical competence*: one's ability to execute the technical aspects of work. Conduct and performance aren't necessarily linked—a person can be technically brilliant and interpersonally dim or interpersonally expert but deficient in technical expertise. The best bosses have solid social *and* business expertise that inspires loyalty and augments the horsepower of their teams. The worst bosses are deficient in one or both competencies—working for a bungling nice guy can be equally as arduous as working for a proficient tyrant.

The Adequate Boss

The interpersonal competence of *adequate bosses* ranges from good enough to great. They have enough emotional intelligence to know how to relate to coworkers in socially acceptable ways that promote smooth working relationships. Adequate bosses aren't perfect, but they're insightful enough to consistently behave in ways that coworkers perceive as respectful. These skills help them maneuver successfully through the inevitable interpersonal rough patches present in any workplace, keeping emotional distress to a minimum.

The Annoying Boss

Like physical irritants that produce minor, transient rashes, *annoying bosses* behave in ways that cause mild, temporary irritation in coworkers. Their annoying behaviors can be a pain, but *the pain is not enough to damage work relationships or organizational functioning.* Annoying bosses are somewhat deficient in the social skills department, and the ways in which they irritate coworkers are endless—they can be loud, long-winded, or late. They can tell too many jokes or belabor too many details. The list goes on, but I won't continue and risk becoming an annoying author. Annoying bosses are perceived as irritating but harmless—we don't take their missteps personally.

The Abrasive Boss

Abrasive is defined as *harsh or rough in manner*, describing the characteristic interpersonal style of *abrasive bosses.* Abrasive bosses rub their coworkers the wrong way, inflicting lasting wounds. *Their behaviors, characterized by aggression, damage work relationships to the point of disrupting organizational functioning.* Coworkers report feeling mistreated when they experience aggressive behavior ranging from mild offense to open attack. The words and actions of abrasive bosses are perceived as harmful and are frequently taken personally, producing intense emotional distress.

The Avoidant Boss

In the case of *avoidant bosses*, coworkers complain not about their presence but about their absence. Avoidant bosses avoid interpersonal contact with coworkers and isolate themselves physically or emotionally (or both) whenever possible. Avoidant bosses hold their coworkers at arm's length, remaining distant, unresponsive, and uninterested in those around them. These bosses will go to great lengths to avoid dealing with potentially difficult interactions whenever possible. Coworker distress results not from abuse but from neglect, which drains motivation and morale. As one coworker of an avoidant boss said, "He acts like we don't exist."

The Aberrant Boss

Aberrant bosses are psychologically abnormal, exhibiting behaviors symptomatic of diagnosable emotional disturbance, such as paranoid, narcissistic, and antisocial (sociopathic) personality disorders. Their psychopathology is reflected in extreme and socially deviant behaviors that wreak havoc on individuals and organizations alike. These behaviors may be premeditated (intentional) and may reflect sadistic tendencies. Examples include the boss who strolled up to his male subordinate's desk, unzipped his pants, and "jokingly" draped his penis in the subordinate's in-box (no joke—this really happened), and the human resource manager who took pleasure in decorating his desk with a filled glass jar labeled "Ashes of Complaining Employees."

Additional Reflections

Adequate bosses treat coworkers (including their subordinates) with respect. They may make unpopular decisions that are hard to swallow, but their interactions with others are consistently courteous. An adequate boss's decision to transfer your group to your company's Siberian division may have a negative impact on your career and family, but if it is made for reasons of business need (as opposed to retaliation) and conveyed respectfully, you're dealing with an adequate boss: "I didn't always agree with his decisions, but he was okay to work for."

Annoying bosses, although irritating, do no harm, unlike abrasive bosses who inflict interpersonal injury. I am frequently challenged on this point: "So what's your definition of harm? Behaviors that harm one person may not even irritate another—so where do you draw the line?" Let's consider that question in light of a specific behavior: the act of interruption, variously perceived as acceptable, annoying, or abrasive, depending on whom you talk to. Personally, I don't mind being interrupted. Yes, it's aggressive behavior, but I enjoy vigorous conversations where participants feel free to challenge each other and express their passion. I also know people who hate being interrupted, who perceive it as rude and controlling. Who is right? Surprise: *everyone* is right, for *perception lies in the eye of the beholder*. I may perceive the interrupter as harmless and relish the prospect of a stimulating conversation, whereas another perceiver may feel harmed and experience resentment. Our differing perceptions are both "right."

So how do we draw the line between harmless and harmful? How do we resolve this perceptual paradox to determine whether a boss is abrasive, or just annoying? Do we poll the workforce for a consensus vote on harmful versus harmless? Flip a coin? Ask the boss in question for his or her opinion? It's a good question, and one that I originally struggled with, but in the absence of any better options, I settled on the following definition of abrasive, or harmful, workplace behavior: *any aggressive interpersonal behavior that causes emotional distress in coworkers sufficient to disrupt organizational functioning.*

In this definition the boss whose aggressive social behaviors disrupt the smooth flow of work is an abrasive boss. This definition allows for variations in work cultures, for what is acceptable in one culture may be destructive in another. Fishmongers at Seattle's Pike Place Market happily shout and throw fish at each other, but I can assure you that shouting and throwing surgical instruments wouldn't be viewed as positively in hospital operating rooms. I've coached many bosses whose behaviors were perfectly appropriate in one work environment (most notably, the military) but proved disastrous in another. Abrasion is defined contextually, in the eyes of the beholder; however, workplace abrasion is distinctive in that it causes sufficient emotional distress to disrupt operations—work no longer works.

Abrasive Boss Identification: A Test

It's time for a test. Your challenge is to identify the type of boss described in this case study. Your options: adequate, annoying, abrasive, avoidant, or aberrant.

Dick and Jane: A Case of Foot in Mouth

Jane had been in her corporate role for only six months when she received a frantic call from Dick, Director of Finance. Dick was scheduled to give a presentation that morning for the company's biggest bigwigs at their annual corporate retreat. Unfortunately, he'd neglected to bring critical documents prepared by Jane's department. He made a frantic call to Jane, begging her to deliver the documents ASAP. Jane agreed to navigate the icy roads up to the mountain resort where they were meeting, and slipped into the back of the conference room. Up on the stage, Dick spotted Jane. Visibly relieved, he called out, "Hey, bitch, what took you so long?!" Dick laughed and Jane froze—had she actually heard what she thought she'd heard? Bitch? *Bitch?!* Jane's mind raced, but unwilling to let anyone see her shock, she handed the papers over without comment and exited.

Jane didn't sleep that night—she tossed and turned, practically shredding her pillow in rage. First thing the next morning she called Dick and requested a meeting. He sounded genuinely happy to hear from her, inviting her over that minute. In cold, measured tones Jane told him that she found being called a bitch unacceptable, and added that she would lodge a formal complaint with the company if he didn't apologize immediately. Dick was totally astounded: "I didn't say that! Gosh—did I say that? I can't believe I would have done something like that." Jane could see that the Dick was sincerely confused—the poor guy was notorious for his social blunders. He promptly and profusely apologized; he obviously felt terrible. Dick then offered to issue a public apology, cc'ing all those who were in attendance at the retreat. Jane declined the offer. Being called a bitch was bad enough–did we need to put it in lights?! Dick repeatedly expressed remorse: "I'm so sorry.... I'm so sorry–please forgive me," Jane accepted his apology and returned to her work, satisfied that Dick would forevermore tread carefully in her presence.

Let's analyze Dick in the context of our boss categories. He clearly doesn't fit the profile of an adequate boss—his grossly disrespectful behavior reflects the emotional intelligence of a walnut. One might be tempted to leap to the conclusion that Dick is a certifiable abrasive boss because of his aggressive behavior; however, *did this behavior cause emotional distress in coworkers* (namely, Jane) *sufficient to disrupt organizational functioning?* Certainly, Dick disrupted Jane's sleep, but did he disrupt the flow of work? The answer is no, and I know this for a fact because I *am* Jane—this actually happened to yours truly. True, I was furious with Dick, but his sincere apology and obvious remorse defused my outrage. I felt no need to complain to the powers that be of his transgression, thereby disrupting their focus. His apology repaired the damage done to our working relationship, and I returned to the salt mines irritated but wound-free. Some might see Dick's behavior as an indicator of underlying mental disorder, but he wasn't crazy—he was clueless. Respected for his technical expertise, he was generally viewed with affection by coworkers (myself included) who accepted his deficient emotional intelligence (or, as I termed it at the time, *emotional stupidity*). He never offended me again.

In this case Dick proved to be an annoying boss. Annoying bosses are fairly common; I suspect that most of us who have been bosses have been annoying bosses at times—I know I have. But Dick was lucky. Another person might not simply have demanded an apology for his outrageous behavior but could instead have charged him with sexual harassment. Such a charge would have disrupted organizational functioning with investigations, adjudications, and penalties, leaving permanent scars on involved individuals and the company.

Abrasive bosses are all too common. Abrasion doesn't discriminate—abrasive bosses may be of any age, sex, color, religion, or ethnicity, but they have one thing in common: aggressive managerial styles that damage work relationships to the point of damaging work. In the next chapter you'll meet an abrasive boss and explore abrasive boss behavior in more detail.

3

Abrasive Boss Behavior

What They Do

I have another confession to make: I didn't want to write this chapter. Having observed abrasive bosses over the past twenty years, I don't find it difficult to describe the characteristics that distinguish them from other bosses. So why was I so resistant? It finally came to me—*I didn't want to write about their behavior for the same reason that my ex-husband never wanted to talk about being attacked by a grizzly bear.* Let me explain: I met Jim in Alaska—a good man and a great wildlife photographer. One day I noticed some strange markings on his upper arm and asked about them. "Oh, a bear did that." I was in shock. He said it in the same tone you or I would use to describe a bug bite. "A bear did that? What do you mean, '*a bear did that*'?!" He hesitated, and then said he really didn't want to go into it. I, trained psychotherapist and loving newlywed, determined to help him work through this seeming posttraumatic avoidance of the event. I also admit that I was dying to hear every gory detail of what promised to be an exciting drama. "You really should talk about it—tell me what happened!"

He reluctantly told the story. A few years back, a then-friend of his had purchased a plane and wanted to give it a spin. Always open to photographic opportunities, Jim signed on. They landed out in the bush, and upon spotting a moose, the friend lifted his rifle (*de rigueur* in bear country), took aim, and fired. Jim shot animals only with a camera and felt deeply disgusted at this unforeseen turn of events, but grudgingly agreed to help cut up the moose to salvage the meat. Wearing a very thick, hooded down parka, he neither heard nor saw the grizzly that approached from behind, scenting warm blood. The bear sunk his teeth into Jim's arm, and Jim reflexively and regretfully cut its throat with the knife he had been using to skin the moose: "I don't like to talk about it," he said, "because I don't want to give bears a bad rap. He was just looking for food and there I was, out there dripping with moose blood like an idiot!" Jim blamed himself for the attack—not the bear. He added that he didn't like to recount the event for fear that it would be sensationalized into yet another "savage attack by rogue bear" tale. I felt deflated somehow, having prepared for a thrilling epic and instead hearing a sad story of a hungry bear just trying to survive.

I didn't want to write this chapter for the same reason that Jim didn't want to tell his story: I didn't want to produce yet another lurid listing of the "crimes" committed by abrasive bosses, chock full of graphic, grisly, and titillating anecdotes along the lines of "Bloodthirsty Bully Boss Goes for the Jugular!" The risk in reading about bear attacks lies in concluding that bears attack because they are evil, in contrast to the reality that bears use aggression to pursue and protect their survival. The same risk lies in reading about boss attacks: it's all too easy to conclude that abrasive bosses display aggression because they are evil or crazed or both. I'll share my thoughts on *why* bears and bosses attack in the following chapter, but for the moment I ask you to suspend judgment as we explore abrasive boss behavior. It won't be easy—at first glance, abrasive bosses and ravenous bears appear equally bloodthirsty.

Mark

Before I describe the distinguishing characteristics of abrasive bosses, I'd like to introduce you to Mark, a mid-thirties manager in a technical services corporation (names and identifying details have been changed to protect the abrasive and nonabrasive in this book). Mark's boss referred him to coaching, stating that he was overly reactive and volatile in his management of subordinates. He was described as sorely lacking in patience and diplomacy, frequently speaking in an inappropriate or offensive manner with subordinates and occasionally with peers. Mark's responses were depicted as "hostile," "threatening," "cold," and "brutal," characterized by name-calling, swearing, criticizing ("ripping"), and by outbursts of temper. Mark used a commanding tone with his coworkers, rarely saying please or thank you. Subordinates and peers portrayed Mark as condescending, proudly demonstrating his superior knowledge, and continually striving to win the "war of the words" by outtalking others. Coworkers felt that he would frequently respond to questions in a tone that implied the questioner was lacking in intelligence for not already knowing the answer.

Coworkers concurred that Mark treated subordinates "like kids," frequently blowing up at them, belittling them, and constantly checking on them. They viewed him as totally uninterested in their needs, stating that he communicated infrequently and failed to advocate for their issues with management and other departments. Their conclusion that they fell low on his priority list resulted in repeated "mutinous" (Mark's term) forays to complain to higher management. At the same time, his superiors described Mark as constantly in need of support, manifested by his continually seeking approval from superiors for the adequacy of his decisions. Regarding strengths, Mark was characterized as motivated, highly intelligent, technically proficient, innovative, and possessed of strong technical business skills. His responsiveness to the requests of others was highly valued, as was his creativity in solving technical problems and his willingness to take on new assignments.

Mark's Achilles' heel as a manager lay with subordinates and, to a lesser degree, with peers whom he perceived as inept, uncooperative, and immature. Mark readily admitted, "I manage up better than down." His anger was most easily ignited by having to deal with his subordinate team, whose members he characterized as immature and difficult. He described them variously as "trouble-makers," "complainers," "whiners," "passive-aggressive," "prideful," and "resistant." He was easily provoked to anger whenever they questioned his decisions, resisted his directives, or performed below his expectations. Underlying his descriptions was a strong theme of impatience with perceived childish incompetence. One legendary blowup, repeatedly recounted, occurred when Mark discovered his team watching a breaking national news alert on a television monitor designated for business use.

Mark often used sports metaphors to describe his team: "You are trying to win the Indy 500 and you are driving a [Volkswagen] Rabbit." Complaints about his team reflected a theme of impatience with slowness, ineptitude, or what he interpreted as passive-aggressive resistance to his leadership. After confronting his team with these perceptions, he reported that they would "just give me a bunch of excuses." Peers who exhibited behaviors that Mark perceived as uncooperative or negligent were also subjected to his anger. He became incensed when peers or subordinates failed to meet a customer's needs to his level of expectation.

Challenges to his knowledge or authority constituted a major theme of provocation for abrasive behavior: "It is repugnant to me when people think they know more than I do and they don't. That is painful—they don't respect me, my knowledge. It's a threat to me." Mark reacted to challenges to his knowledge or authority with aggression, which took the form, as he described it, of "rattling the cage" of the offending party: "[You have to] grab them by the face mask and rattle their cage. There are certain types of people who are motivated by fear; others who are self-motivated, who respond to the carrot."

Mark's management strategy involved instilling fear in order to motivate employees. In the course of coaching, Mark would come to describe this as his "bazooka" strategy, designed to "blast" a person out of resistance and into action. Mark did this only with those he thought could tolerate it. He described one employee who, although a "bit of a whiner," was perceived by Mark as having "a self-doubting personality": "I never grabbed him by the face mask—that would damage him." Instead, he resorted to lecturing such coworkers "just like kids." Referring to a resistant subordinate, he commented: "I can send five-year-olds to their room. I wanted to give the bastard a time- out." In response to the aforementioned television-watching episode, Mark lambasted his team in a manner they later described as that of an angry parent lecturing little children.

Mark rarely responded abrasively to superiors, employing logic and diplomacy to overcome perceived resistance to his recommendations. However, when Mark experienced resistance from peers or perceived them as incompetent, particularly on issues of customer care, he would leave scathing voice mails or immediately e-mail his complaints to their superiors. Assessing his management style, Mark commented, "I have a certain affinity for the military operational ass-kicking framework. . . . You don't make soufflé on the front line of battle." He added that he had never received any management training: "I was thrown in to run a team." In describing his management interventions, Mark relied almost entirely on sports and military metaphors, using terms such as "grab their face mask," "rattle their cage," "bazooka," "bash," "beat," "blast," "sabotage," "mutiny," and "throw down the gauntlet." Describing his management objectives he said: "I play to win. I give 110 percent every day. Some coaches are nice, but they don't win the Super Bowl. . . . [When you are] driving a Rabbit [at the Indianapolis 500], you are not going to win. So you can get mad, or you can decide to do what it takes."

The Big Five

Mark's KITA (or as he termed it, "bazooka") approach to management inflicted deep interpersonal wounds. Mark exhibited the five primary behavioral characteristics of abrasive bosses, resorting to overcontrol, threats, public humiliation, condescension, and overreaction in his interactions with coworkers. When I first started coaching abrasive bosses, I was struck by the seemingly endless array of aversive behaviors they displayed—behaviors that alienated their coworkers. But over the years I realized that these behaviors were actually variations on five themes. Let's listen to the themes that characterize abrasive bosses from the perspective of their coworkers:

1. Overcontrol

"It's all command and control—it's always *just do it.* There's no discussion or input."

"He's a total micromanager. He treats us like kids instead of adults. I've got a babysitter for a boss."

"Her micromanaging destroys initiative. No one is willing to make a decision, because if you do, you can be sure she'll change it."

"He never asks questions—he just issues orders. It's win-lose instead of a win-win collaboration."

"Don't ever disagree on anything—if you do, you're doomed."

"You'd better do things exactly the way he wants them or he'll eat you for lunch."

"He has the power and he never lets you forget who is king—his department is his domain."

"It's always *do this, do that* and never 'please,' 'thank you,' 'would you.'"

"She'll interrupt you anytime, anywhere—you'll be on the phone and she'll cut in and demand that you hang up and give her instant attention."

"He doesn't share his reasoning, won't give his rationale for decisions. It's just *do it.*'"

"If it's his idea, it's a good idea, and doesn't have to be substantiated. If it's your idea, you have to kill yourself proving it."

"He makes you feel like a slave/peon/nobody/his whipping boy."

"I've never seen him apologize. He thinks it would diminish his authority."

2. Threats

"He's the 'my way or the highway' type."

"When he gets worked up, he threatens to sack the whole team."

" 'Heads are going to roll' —it's like working for the Queen of Hearts!"

"He's always saying, 'You'll do this or there will be consequences.' "

"She told someone that if they didn't like the way she ran things, she'd be happy to write them a reference."

"He'll get right up in your face like he's ready for a face-off."

"He enforces through fear—'If this doesn't get done, your job is history.' "

"It's 'shape up or ship out.' "

"If I make the slightest error, she threatens to write me up. If she makes the same error, she just laughs it off. There's a double standard with a single-edged sword— the edge for my throat."

"People feel threatened all the time—'If you don't like it, get out!' "

3. Public Humiliation

"He yells at people and belittles them out where everyone can hear."

"She has no qualms about making a person look bad in front of others."

"He sits back and lets everyone talk, and then if he disagrees, he explains why everyone is wrong."

"He will tell you what he thinks you're doing wrong—right in the hallway—in front of others."

"He'll make derogatory comments about someone so that everyone knows who's on his shit list."

"She criticizes the entire team for the mistakes of a few, and it's not hard to figure out who she's targeting."

"He badmouths other people to me—makes me wonder what he says about me to them."

"If you dare to question him, he'll debate you until you're totally humiliated—crushed."

"He can be really intimidating. Everyone is afraid of getting hammered in front of the group—they clam up."

4. Condescension

"He assumes everyone is stupid and treats us like third graders."

"Her tone conveys 'I'm bright and right—you're slow and stupid.'"

"He prides himself on his demonstrating his brilliance. He enjoys putting you in your place, like a cat toying with a mouse."

"She always talks down to people like she's the only one that knows anything."

"He doesn't have time for you—he's always got to show how important he is."

"He'll zap you with these e-mails written in a very simplistic manner, implying that you're dense."

"He's famous for rolling his eyeballs or snorting in contempt."

"She acts like she's God's gift to the company—a total know-it-all."

"He batters people with questions. He quizzes them like they're absolute clods."

"His biggest downfall is that he thinks too much of himself and too little of us. He should be more aware."

"He's threatened that others will think they're smarter than he is."

5. Overreaction

"He's incredibly impatient—if you don't immediately understand what he's asking for, he'll come unglued."

"He makes snap judgments—makes assumptions and leaps to conclusions without investigating."

"It's all knee-jerk decision making—he has no interest in talking things out."

"The smallest thing can set him off—he'll slam his fist on the table to make his point."

"She's got a short fuse—the slightest frustration can set her off."

"Everything has to be a crisis—he's always in panic mode."

"His impatience is legendary—one misstep and he'll fly off the handle."

" 'Quick to convict'—that describes him."

"When you try to tell him about a problem, he jumps the gun and blames us."

"She won't let you finish a sentence before she leaps in with her solution."

"He's easily angered, and it can be directed at anyone. He forgets it an hour later, but the target remembers it forever. He has inflicted deep personal wounds."

"We've all learned to keep our mouths shut, because if you challenge him he'll blow up."

There they are, the Big Five indicators of an abrasive boss: overcontrol, threats, public humiliation, condescension, and overreaction. Abrasive bosses may possess only one of these five characteristics, but it takes only one to alienate coworkers and disrupt the smooth flow of work. This is not to say that abrasive bosses don't engage in other aversive behaviors, but I have yet to encounter an abrasive boss who didn't display at least one of the Big Five. Here are some additional abrasive behaviors that I've observed with less frequency:

Aggressive Language

"He'll yell at people—'*Shut up!*'"

"He's always calling people '*worthless*', '*stupid*,' or '*lazy*.'"

"She'll say, '*How could you possibly be so stupid to think that?!*'"

"The profanity is terrible when he gets worked up—you need a heat shield."

"He writes really nasty e-mails, very insulting."

"There's lots of crude language. It really puts people off."

"She yells at whoever gets in her way. It's hard to come to work."

Hostile Humor

"He thinks it's funny to imply we're goofing off when he can see we're not—'*When are you guys going to get off your butts and get to work?*'"

"He calls me '*asshole*'—'*Hey, asshole, how ya doin'?*' He claims it's a term of affection."

"On payday he told us in all seriousness that our pay-checks would be late, and then he whipped them out of his drawer at the last minute. He thought it was hilarious, but it's nothing to joke about."

Favoritism and Discrimination

"He plays favorites. If you agree with everything he says, you're in with the 'in crowd.'"

"She goes after the ones she doesn't like and lets the others get away with murder."

"He's the nicest guy in the world to his superiors, but he treats us like chopped liver."

"Unless you're a member of the 'right' religion, you don't have a chance in hell."

"If she doesn't like you, you go on her blacklist—she won't even talk to you."

"Don't get on his bad side. If you do, you're in the doghouse forever—there's no coming back."

As I noted earlier, the ways in which abrasive bosses rub their coworkers raw are infinite. Abrasive bosses can be guilty of any "un" in the book: unsupportive, undependable, unthinking, untrustworthy, unwise, unpredictable, and most of all, uncaring. There's no special definition of abrasive workplace behavior—essentially, *any behavior considered abrasive in day-to-day social interaction can constitute abrasive workplace behavior*. There's another term for these behaviors: they're just plain *rude*. And all the abovementioned behaviors, including the Big Five and the other aforementioned "un"s, share a single common factor: they all communicate disrespect. It's the leading emotional lesion I encounter in my conversations with the working wounded—disrespect. It resonates through every interview:

"I've never been treated this way in my life—with such disrespect."

"After you've been disrespected for so long you start to lose respect for yourself."

"When you come to work you leave your self-respect at the door and hope to pick it up on your way out."

Diagnosis: Bastard?

Now that you've met Mark and analyzed his behavior in the light of the Big Five, are you ready to render your diagnosis: *chronic bastardism, evil type?* As I discovered, the bully book authors reflexively leap to the conclusion that abrasive bosses must be evil or crazy or both. But before you move to convict, I ask you to pause and instead consider what motivates bosses to overcontrol, threaten, humiliate, condescend, and overreact. What purpose do these behaviors serve? First, listen to their coworkers:

"His voice will elevate, he will take a more aggressive stance, moving into your zone of comfort to intimidate you."

"He'll try to intimidate you with his tantrums. Some guys are scared to death of him."

"He's a big guy, with a commanding presence. He uses that to intimidate you."

"His attitude is, 'Why should I spend time on the touchy-feely if I can intimidate you into getting the product out the door?'"

"She'll glare at you to intimidate you."

"He tends to lead by scaring people—he motivates through intimidation."

"Everyone is intimidated. They don't want to be humiliated in front of the group."

"He badgers people, intimidates them. He makes it clear that he's dominant and they have to obey."

The Big Five behaviors serve one common purpose: they *intimidate*. Overcontrol *shows you who's boss* (whether or not you report to the individual), and threats communicate the cost of forgetting that fact. Humiliation *belittles* you, *diminishes* you, making you *less than* your boss. Condescension teaches you your position in relation to the boss—you are *inferior* to your *superior*; you are *lower* on the totem pole. And overreaction *shakes you up* and then *puts you down*, in case you're getting too uppity. In short the Big Five *put you in your place*—and that place is *down*, down under the abrasive boss's control.

Abrasive bosses are sounding more and more like bastards and bitches, aren't they? Well, hold on to your horses, because this boss whisperer is going to ask you to do exactly what I do—I'm going to ask you to *read* abrasive bosses' behaviors and consider the meaning of those behaviors. I'm going to ask you to put yourself in their shoes and try to understand why they do what they do; why they are driven to put their coworkers down. Brace yourself—*I'm going to ask you to empathize with abrasive bosses.* I'm going to ask you to get into their shoes to discern why they ride roughshod over their coworkers, using intimidation to secure submission. You'll find it's all about business—the business of survival.

4

Bears, Bosses, and Business

Survival Through Dominance

When people get wind of the fact that I'm in the business of boss whispering, they frequently ask how I'm able to do this work: "*Aren't you afraid to work with them?*" This question implies that abrasive bosses will attack anyone they encounter in their territory, a belief also held of large predators in the wild. In the course of my professional life I've had the opportunity to observe animal behavior in a variety of habitats, from grizzly bears traversing Arctic tundra to abrasive bosses roaming their departments. If you're going to tame an abrasive boss, you'll be at an advantage if you're familiar with the laws of nature observed in my interactions with *Ursus arctos horribilis* and *Bossus abrasivus*. Here's what I've learned:

Laws of the Wild (Workplace)

1. They just want to go about their business.
2. Their business is survival.
3. Dominance pays.
4. They defend against threats to survival with aggression.
5. You'll pay if you get in their way.

1. They Just Want to Go About Their Business

I encountered grizzly bears long before my first meeting with an abrasive boss, so I'll start with a bear-generated lesson. After completing my master's degree in clinical social work, I moved to Seattle, only to discover that this particular ecosystem was overrun with members of the same profession competing for very few positions. I decided to migrate to better job-hunting grounds and purchased a ticket on the Alaska ferry to the Last Frontier. I will confess that I arrived in Alaska with certain prejudices about grizzly bears. In those days I firmly believed that if I stumbled on one of these furred individuals, said bear would take an immediate interest in me as a menu item and promptly attack. Abrasive bosses are subjected to this same prejudice in that the common myth holds that they too attack at first sight.

I was plodding away on a backpacking trip north of the Arctic Circle when terrain forced a turn into a hidden valley. There, on a ridge only a few hundred feet away, I suddenly became aware of three berry-picking grizzlies, a sow and two large cubs (well, they weren't exactly *picking* the berries, but it was clear that some form of berry ingestion was under way). Did I run for my life? Did I collapse into a quivering clod as wilderness experts advise? Not exactly: I came, I saw, I froze. I was transfixed by these magnificent creatures industriously going about the business of survival. Then, to my great surprise, I discovered I was miffed. Yes, *miffed*. Was I not a member of mighty *Homo sapiens*, apex predator (otherwise known as *boss*) of the civilized world? Did I not merit even a moment's notice by these bears, bosses of the uncivilized world?

The answer, as evidenced by their continued berry picking, was a resounding no. Contrary to my beliefs, not only did they not attack, but worse, they totally ignored me—they had more important business to attend to. In this most humbling moment of wilderness revelation, I realized that these grizzlies, like all other residents of the animal kingdom, *just wanted to go about their business*. And it was clear that on this particular day the business of berry picking yielded a superior return on investment when weighed against the costs in time and energy (and perhaps taste) of attacking me.

I have observed the same phenomenon in my encounters with abrasive bosses. Contrary to popular belief, they don't automatically attack any coworker who enters their field of vision. They, like these bears, just *want to go about their business*—you will be tolerated if you don't get in their way, and you'll risk serious injury if you do. Coworkers will tell me that abrasive bosses can be very agreeable people when they're not in their boss roles: "Outside of work, he can be a really nice person—but when he's the boss, he's a bear." In other words, they can be quite amenable away from their territory, but if you get in their way, there's hell to pay.

2. Their Business Is Survival

Think of survival as a business venture: the primary business objective of all living organisms. Achieving this objective allows organisms to reproduce and evolve, thus enjoying life and evading extinction. If you're lucky enough to be a member of a species that evolved digestive tracts and reproductive organs, you may enjoy the added benefits of a full stomach, hot sex, and other assorted perks that make Survival, Inc. an attractive enterprise. This same principle applies to members of *Homo sapiens* in their workplace habitats—those who demonstrate fitness will survive to support themselves, their offspring, and their organization. If you're lucky enough to be a member of a company that has evolved highly successful business processes, you may enjoy the added benefits of a fat financial portfolio, hot mergers, and other assorted perks that make the business of survival highly rewarding.

I listen carefully to bosses and their coworkers, and over the years I have learned that people who work for a living naturally understand this concept of business as survival. Business language reflects this naturalistic understanding of the harsh realities of business. Work is a *rat race*, where we *run with the dogs* and *swim with the sharks*. We compete for *top-dog* status so that we can *lead the pack* and avoid being the *underdog*. We *bark* orders and *dog* issues as we *fight tooth and nail* to reach the top of the *food chain*. We *butt heads* and *lock horns*. We fight internal *turf battles* and *defend our territory* against external threats to achieve market dominance. We *fight to the death* to keep from being *eaten alive*. And if we work for an abrasive boss, we can get *chewed on* or risk *getting our heads bitten off*. We talk about the cold, cruel *dog-eat-dog* world of business, a ruthlessly competitive environment where companies fight to survive, thrive, and dominate. We face hostile business climates swarming with threats of rising costs, restrictive regulation, and fierce competition. Although Darwin's evolutionary theory of natural selection is still contested by many, I have yet to encounter a businessperson who doesn't accept that in the evolution of successful companies, *only the fit survive*.

How is fitness defined in the business world? In nature, fitness is determined by one's environment. Organisms that evolve adaptations guaranteeing their success in one ecosystem may, like the proverbial fish out of water, fail miserably if transplanted to another. Similarly, employees possessing skills that allow them to flourish in one line of business may not survive if transferred to another. By the way, when you wander around companies you won't hear people talking about *fitness*—they refer to it as *competence*. Employers select applicants for desired "key competencies" and provide ongoing training to develop employee competence. Through the process of natural selection the most competent will be promoted to ascend the corporate ladder, or as we say in the animal world, attain *dominance*.

But what about the boss who, from your perspective, is profoundly incompetent? What about the bosses who rise through the ranks because of favoritism, nepotism, or some other "ism" that has nothing to do with their actual competence to perform the work at hand? If you look closely at each of these situations, it becomes obvious that fitness is defined differently in different environments. Consider the employee who meets his boss's every need (also known as the *kiss-up* or *brown-noser*) but dodges responsibility whenever the boss's back is turned. His incompetence as a team member grates on his peers, but his competence in catering upward renders him of great value to his boss. In many family businesses, family members are perceived as innately more competent because of their presumed primary loyalty to the family and assumed trustworthiness. In this environment, superior competence is determined not by sweat, but by blood, which is believed to be thicker than water.

3. Dominance Pays

At Survival, Inc. dominance pays big dividends and a better salary, whether in cash or carrion. Dominance means that you've achieved top-dog status—you're the alpha wolf of your pack, the lead horse of your herd, the boss of your team. You are at the top of your particular heap, or hierarchy, and the benefits are many. Sociologist Allan Mazur (2005) defines a dominance hierarchy as

> a fairly persistent, unequal ranking of members in terms of power, influence, and access to valued prerogatives. This definition applies as well to fish and nonhuman primates as to people. High-ranking individuals do pretty much what they want and influence others in the group. Subordinate individuals have little influence, are constrained in their choices, and are limited to resources that are allowed them by—or escape the attention of—those more dominant [p. 7].

Dominance is a darn good deal, no matter what your species. Here the objective is not just to survive, but to consistently *win*, to be stronger, larger, faster, and smarter in order to outdo other group members, rise through the ranks, and win priority access to valued resources. What ape, naked or otherwise, doesn't dream of being top banana? But as humans, our interests extend beyond bananas, beyond the tangible fruits of dominance such as company cars and corner offices. We also seek the psychological benefits of dominance: to be accorded respect (esteem) as well as compliance with (deference to) our wishes. If you're dominant, *you* give the orders. You call the shots instead of taking them. You run the show as others work to fulfill your directives.

So how does one attain dominance? You have to compete and *win*, proving that you are better than the average bear. You have to meet your environment's criteria for fitness, and then you have to prove yourself fitter than those around you. To be dominant, you can't just be fit—you have to be *superfit*. And to rise through the ranks of organizational hierarchies, you can't just be competent—you have to be *supercompetent*, according to their criteria. You have to be able to leap tall objectives in a single bound and respond faster than the speeding bullet points coming at you. Listen to these bosses as they speak of their need to be dominant:

> "I want to move the project ahead. I just want to be successful. . . I want to consistently hit those high numbers, get fitter and leaner, and make sure that we perform at our top capacity. . . . I don't want us to just survive—I want us to thrive."

> "You are trying to win the Indy 500. . . I play to win. I give 110 percent every day. Some coaches are nice, but they don't win the Super Bowl."

> "Weakness is losing your credibility. Winning means being very powerful."

> "I have always been in control since I was young. I always had control in my life. . . . I am a driver. I cannot stand it when people just sit there and projects fail. It's gut-wrenching."

Organizational dominance in human companies (also known as *bossdom*) is officially designated by position. Upon entry into a formal (official) hierarchy, you are given a title that instantaneously broadcasts your status, from top executive to lowly mailroom clerk. Humans are the only group-living animals to evolve official hierarchies, as evidenced by their ability to create organizational charts. However, all group-living animals compete for personal status in unofficial, face-to-face dominance contests to determine who is the coolest cat (or dog). Here, rank can be determined by a variety of attributes, such as size, strength, appearance, intelligence, and behavior. Dominant bighorn rams will have—you guessed it—the *biggest horns*, and dominant third-grade girls will display the *best-dressed Barbies*. Dominant individuals display distinctive behaviors, discovered from research on dominance hierarchies across primate species. Be you furred or naked ape, here are some specific behavioral indicators of high and low rank, summarized from Mazur's *Biosociology of Dominance and Deference* (2005):

High Rank	*Low Rank*
Priority access to resources (food, water, space)	Secondary access to resources
At the center of group activity	Peripheral to group activity
Exerts authority	Defers to authority
Confident demeanor	Anxious demeanor
Erect posture	Diminished posture
Displays dominant gestures (lunges, bites, barks, stares)	Displays submissive gestures (withdraws, avoids eye contact)

For your further edification and entertainment, I offer some human-specific dominance behaviors described in Mazur's book. See if you observe them in action during the next powwow of your company's "chiefs":

- Dominant individuals set the pace and mood for conversations, while low-status members mirror the dominant person's tone, facial expressions, and timing.

- High-status individuals introduce and terminate major topics of conversation.
- High-status individuals interrupt more often.
- High-status individuals ask more questions.
- Suggestions made by low-status individuals are ignored more often.
- Most arguments are dominance contests.

4. They Defend Against Threats to Survival

Attaining dominance is only part of the story—you have to *keep* it to stay on top. And if any in your pack threaten your right to dominance, you have to *put them down* and *keep them in their place*. Woe to the upstart walrus who dares to defy the dominant bull of the herd. And woe to the subordinate employee who threatens the boss with inadequate performance—with incompetence. More often than not, a boss's survival depends on the fitness of his or her team; *team members must perform competently if the boss is to maintain his or her dominant status*. Anything that jeopardizes dominance, such as walrus insubordination or coworker incompetence, falls into the category of threat. Threats to one's dominance are dangerous, and organisms have evolved a wide array of physical and behavioral mechanisms to defend against such dangers.

If you hang out at a hospital long enough, chances are that you'll hear about a surgeon notorious for his abrasive behavior. In the exercise of empathy, let us step into his surgical booties and see his world through the lens of threat, fear, and defense. In the surgical domain, fitness is determined by a surgeon's ability to "fix" patients. Competent surgeons fix, whereas incompetent surgeons fillet. Surgeons, like grizzlies, *just want to go about their business*, in this case the business of fixing patients. However, unlike grizzlies' competence, a surgeon's competence is partially dependent on others. Woe to the surgical assistant who proffers the wrong instrument and *gets in the way of business*—that assistant's incompetence is a direct (if unintended) *threat* to the surgeon's competence. And keep in mind that the stakes are very high. We're not just berry picking here—this is life-or-death stuff. The threat of being rendered incompetent by those the surgeon depends on can provoke extreme anxiety—*fear* of failure—which in turn stimulates extreme *aggression designed to defend against the threat of incompetence*. It's at this moment that abrasive surgeons shout, swear, or act out in ways that others find intimidating:

> "Her mistake cost us precious minutes. I blew up at her because I was so angry. I started shouting and swearing—I knew my behavior was out of line, but I was reacting to the fact that her screwup jeopardized my ability to help this patient. I had to fight back for my patient's sake, and I didn't want to get a reputation for botching things up."

The dynamic of defensive behavior (which I will from here on refer to as the *survival dynamic*) follows a fairly predictable course in all animals, including humans. It starts with the perception of *threat*, which gives rise to *fear* (or *anxiety*), which in turn mobilizes one or more *defense* mechanisms. It's a simple formula: *threat* → *fear* → *defense*. The assistant's incompetence proved a *threat* to our surgeon's competence; the surgeon then experienced *anxiety* over the survival of his status as a competent physician and *defended* against the threat with aggression, verbally flogging his coworker into competence (or so he hoped). Simply put, threat provokes fear which activates defense. Listen to these bosses as they voice their anxieties over perceived incompetence:

> "Laziness—I cannot stand people that are lazy—that pushes my buttons more than anything else."

"I struggle with people who can't move ahead. I have the patience of a wounded rhino. I can't deal with people who stand in the way of my vision—they waste my time."

"I was totally frustrated when they resisted, when they said, 'It's already been done and it didn't work.' I blew. Come hell or high water, I will make it work."

"He gets this look in his eyes—if you flinch or show weakness, if you don't deliver, he will go for you."

"He is dominant. It's like watching a Rottweiler—he will take them down, with his paw on their neck, and then let them up and see if they obey."

"Don't bark at me. If you want to argue with me, we'll have an argument. I have no problem with butting heads, but my intent is always to win. I will win."

"I have trouble when people put blocks in front of me. I am ruthless; I hang them out to dry."

You'll Pay If You Get in Their Way

I suspect that this fifth law of the wild (workplace) doesn't need a lot of explanation. The fact that you're reading this book suggests that you've already paid a price for getting in the way of an abrasive boss, or you've observed others pay that price. If you get in the way of a bear trying to go about its business, you'll risk getting growled at, bitten, or digested. If you get in the way of an abrasive boss trying to go about his or her business, you'll risk getting barked at, chewed on, or roughed up. In each case you'll sustain wounds that will threaten your survival in the wild or the workplace, up to and including termination. If you threaten an abrasive boss's ability to achieve his or her objectives, you may be starved through lack of psychological or professional support, suffocated by overcontrol, or pay the ultimate price, namely, employment extinction. To summarize: you'll pay if you get in the way of an abrasive boss. You'll be roughed up or rubbed out—abrasion hurts.

Socratic Whispering

Coaching conversations with my abrasive clients helped me see the threat → fear → defense dynamic driving their aggressive behavior. I wanted them to see it too, because people can't change what they don't see. But to make them see, I'd have to find a way that didn't threaten them. Interpretive lecturing wouldn't work here: "When you yell at coworkers what you are really doing is mobilizing aggression to maintain your dominance (and thus control) to ward off the threat of coworker (and ultimately your own) incompetence." Yeah, right. That would have the same effect as my father telling me the real reason I didn't want to come home for spring vacation—it would provoke defensiveness. I could only imagine a client's response: "What do you mean—*my incompetence*?! I'm not incompetent! I hold one of the highest positions in this company! And what kind of incompetent coach are you to say something so stupid?!" (*Score: Boss, 100; Coach, 0.*)

I settled on a technique that I call *Socratic whispering*, based on the Socratic method. Socrates believed that all humans have knowledge and that all it took to access that knowledge were the right questions. The Socratic method of teaching focuses on asking rather than telling: questions generate hypotheses, which are tested by further questions. I rely on Socratic whispering to help abrasive bosses see what they do, to help them develop insight into their aggressive behavior. Here's an example of the method applied to a client struggling to metabolize a massive dose of feedback from his distressed coworkers:

Boss: All right, *all right*—I've *got* it. I see that my behavior causes problems. It hurts and demoralizes my employees, makes me look bad, and focuses their attention on their anger with me instead of on the tasks at hand—I see that. But what do I do to change it? How do I get people to do what I want them to do without blasting them?

Coach: Your feedback showed that your employees deeply resent being called "stupid" or "idiots."

Boss: I only do it when I'm frustrated.

Coach: Do you know *why* you do it?

Boss: No—well, come to think of it, I do. I feel like they've really screwed up on a project and that they need to realize that and that blasting them a bit will get them to realize that they've got to shape up.

Coach: So you do it to be sure that they understand that they've made a serious mistake?

Boss: Yes—but I suppose they already know that. I don't suppose it helps to call them names.

Coach: Why not?

Boss: Because it's clear from the feedback that it alienates them—that they get resentful. I didn't need the feedback to tell me that. I can see it when I do it.

Coach: Why then, knowing that calling them names will alienate them, knowing that it is counterproductive, do you think you still do it?

Boss: I just get so ticked that I lose it. I just start yelling.

Coach: What are you ticked about?

Boss: I'm afraid that they just plain don't have what it takes to do the job and that the whole project will fail.

Coach: So you're afraid that they, the project, and ultimately *you* will fail, and you yell at them as a way of dealing with that fear, to defend against the prospect of failure?

Boss: Exactly. I can see how stupid it looks, but that's what happens. So what am I supposed to do? How do I get people to do what I want if I don't blast them?

See how it works? I just ask questions—no lecturing. I've found Socratic whispering to be a very effective method for getting abrasive bosses to see *what* they do and *why* they do it. If there is to be any hope of changing their management style, they have to see their behavior in order to develop insight into the psychological forces driving that behavior. However, because most bosses have had little or no exposure to psychology, much less psychoanalytic theory, I take a more didactic approach, although still in the context of Socratic inquiry. To accomplish this, I first seek my client's permission to pontificate: "Would you be willing to endure a very short lecture titled 'My Four-Minute View of How the World Works'?" Despite a few rolling eyeballs, I have yet to be refused:

> *Coach:* What two things are people most afraid of? More than anything else in the world, what two things do people fear most?
>
> *Boss:* Dying? Getting fired? Going bankrupt? [*Other typical responses are divorce, illness, harm to children, taxes, and yes, public speaking.*]
>
> *Coach:* You're really close. Let me get a little psychoanalytic on you. Freud believed that there were two things people feared above all: *loss of life* and *loss of love*. He called these fears *annihilation anxiety* and *abandonment anxiety*— fear of loss of life and fear of loss of love. Let's consider loss of life. We're not talking just about loss of physical life, say, through illness or accident. It could be loss of or injury to one's professional life through job termination or demotion. Or loss of economic life through bankruptcy. Loss of love could also occur in various ways: for instance, through death of a loved one, divorce, rejection by a friend, loss of a colleague's respect, or loss of the approval of an employer. What fears do you think people experience when they are demoted? Perhaps loss of their professional life, of their career, because they might be afraid the next step is termination. And loss of the respect of others.

Boss: Right—loss of love—they might feel abandoned because their boss has lost respect for them.

Coach: We're not that distant from other animals in that their greatest fear is loss of life (annihilation), and in higher species, loss of love (or at least connection) with parent, mate, or offspring (abandonment). When a caribou spots a grizzly bear, it perceives a *threat*—the bear could kill it and eat it. Upon perceiving the threat, the caribou experiences *fear* and tries to figure out a way to defend against annihilation. What two defense options do organisms have when confronted with a threat?

Boss: That's easy—fight or flight. They can either flee or fight for their life.

Coach: I believe it's the same with people. When faced with a threat, whether threat of annihilation or abandonment, people can flee (withdraw), or they can fight (attack). For instance, if people fear they are going to be demoted, they can withdraw by quitting, or they can fight the threat by attacking their boss's capabilities. Or they can try to defend against the threat by working harder or longer. Let's apply this thinking to the time you called your employees "stupid." You just told me that you were anxious that they wouldn't be able to complete the project and that you would end up failing. What was the threat to you?

Boss: Loss of life, because my job might get annihilated, and loss of love, because I would lose the respect of upper management if I couldn't deliver.

Coach: And did that create anxiety?

Boss: Yeah, I was afraid that both things could happen.

Coach: And how did you try to protect—to defend—yourself against these threats?

Boss: I yelled at my people to get their act together.

Coach: So you were afraid that you would fail, and in response to that fear you yelled at your people.

You *saw* a threat, *felt* anxiety, and *defended* yourself by attacking your team.

Boss: That about describes it.

(Score: Boss, 1,000; Coach, 1,000.)

Crusaders for Competence

Just like bears, bosses just want to go about their business. Their business is survival, and dominance pays big dividends in terms of greater control and access to resources. Bears and bosses will defend against threats to their survival—neither wants to be rendered incompetent as they struggle to survive. And if other organisms in a bear's or boss's territory get in the way of this business of survival, they'll pay. As one abrasive boss eloquently expressed it: "Is this job survivable? I have done a good job. If I feel threatened, in any way, shape, or form, I will come out swinging. This is survival, tooth and nail."

In the animal and human business domains you'll observe two management styles: *affiliative* or *aggressive*, otherwise known as motivation by carrot or by stick. A lot has been written about leadership, but as far as I can tell, it all boils down to a basic formula: dominance is achieved through love (affiliation) or fear (aggression). Leaders attain and maintain dominance because we love what they do *for* us or fear what they do *to* us. The following observation was shared by a client: "A mentor once said you can motivate people by being a sheepherder or a shepherd. A sheepherder uses dogs to nip at the heels of the sheep to get them to move along. A shepherd raises his cane and the sheep follow."

You'll have to check with your local sheep whisperer to verify the veracity of this statement, but it does a decent job of describing the two modes of motivation: to be pushed by fear or pulled by love. Abrasive bosses push with fear. They motivate through in *timid* ation—they make you *timid*. For them, intimidation is the optimal motivational strategy—they don't see any other way to motivate. They're proud of their approach and are convinced that aggression is justified: "I don't have time to coddle people who can't make a decision. I have to kick ass—it's faster."

The surgeon mentioned earlier felt his aggression was not only justified but required. Wasn't it his duty to resort to whatever measures were necessary to motivate others into competence? Beyond expedience, many abrasive bosses consider their painfully direct approaches to be honorable for their honesty:

> "It's a difference in style. I've been told to soften up
> my communications, to be more polite, less blunt.
> I've fought that, because I don't believe in sugarcoat-
> ing the truth. A lot of people can't handle the truth,
> can't present the truth. I don't want to sugarcoat the
> truth, to be someone so politically correct that when
> I chastise people they feel good about it."

In this boss's view, softening aggression meant being untruthful and underhanded; blunt force was the only honorable approach. I was surprised to discover that many abrasive bosses believe their aggressive behaviors are not only necessary and justified—amazingly, they believe that they're *honorable*. They consider themselves crusaders for competence, viewing their behavior as necessary, ethical, and admirable. Many of these individuals take pride in communicating without tact or consideration for others' emotions. They feel that threats to competence can be overcome only through force, by aggressively wielding the sword of intimidation. But they don't really wield the sword—they just rattle it.

Actual Aggression Versus Threat Display

I have baboons to thank for my insights on sword rattling. I was watching a documentary on baboon behavior that showed the dominant baboon (I'll call him BossBoon) rampaging through his troupe, intimidating members with his shrieks, near-miss charges, and other assorted aggressive gestures. The narrator termed these behaviors *threat displays*. These displays threatened aggression, but they didn't constitute actual aggression. In other words, BossBoon's gestures *threatened* physical harm without *doing* physical harm. From the biological perspective:

> An individual is said to act aggressively if its apparent intent is to inflict physical injury on a member of its species. An individual acts dominantly if its apparent intent is to achieve or maintain high status—that is, to obtain power, influence, or valued prerogatives—over a conspecific [member of the same species]. Rodents typically dominate aggressively, but that is not true among the higher primates [Mazur, 2005, p. 109].

In other words, animals occupying lower branches on the zoological tree will resort to actual physical aggression to exert their dominance—they'll literally bite off each other's heads. Higher primates will rely primarily on threat displays to attain and maintain dominance, rattling banana branches or swords, depending on the species. And interestingly, the higher you go on the evolutionary tree, the greater the reliance on affiliative, rather than aggressive, behaviors to maintain dominance. Mazur compares the more evolved dominance strategies of higher primates to the primitive aggression of lower primates:

> Humans usually establish and maintain status rank without physical fights, aggressive threats, or overt gestures of submission. . . . Lower primates are limited, repetitive, and stereotypic in their displays; high primates are more flexible, using diverse and novel forms of expression. . . . Bonobos seem even more tolerant [than chimpanzees and gorillas] and perhaps are second only to humans in the civility of their normal status interactions [pp. 61, 63].

Higher primates possess the capacity to use affiliative, civil-(ized) behaviors to maintain their dominance through respect rather than intimidation. This difference in approaches signifies the primary difference between adequate and abrasive bosses: adequate bosses display *respect* for their coworkers, whereas abrasive bosses display *aggression*. Abrasive bosses take the more primitive approach, using aggression to intimidate coworkers into compliance and—as they see it—competence.

This difference between actual aggression and threat displays in baboons triggered another blinding flash of the obvious regarding bosses: abrasive bosses see their intimidating tactics as *threats* of aggression, rather than *acts* of aggression. They see themselves as all bark and no bite and are astounded when they are confronted with the deep emotional wounds caused by their behavior. Consider how these abrasive bosses react to coworker feedback on their aggressive displays:

> "I can't believe they took what I said literally. I didn't have any intention of actually firing them. I just wanted to jolt them into action."

> "It kills me to think that people think I'm out to get them. I'm just trying to get the job done—it's nothing personal."

> "I'm blown away. I knew there were a few negative opinions floating around out there, but nothing like this. They think I'm pure evil."

BossBoon didn't inflict physical harm with his threat displays, and one has to wonder if the other baboons took his behaviors personally—I doubt it. But there's no doubt that the threat displays of abrasive bosses are taken very personally, inflicting severe emotional wounds on coworkers and companies. As I mentioned at the beginning of this chapter, bears and bosses (and now baboons) display certain similar characteristics in their struggle for survival:

1. They just want to go about their business.
2. Their business is survival.

3. Dominance pays.

4. They defend against threats to survival with aggression.

5. You'll pay if you get in their way.

But unlike adequate bosses, who rely on civilized manage-ment and disciplinary mechanisms to defend against threats to competence, abrasive bosses rely on overcontrol, threats, public humiliation, condescension, and overreaction to manage oth-ers. Their distinctive threat displays serve to *put people down* (dominate) and *shake people up* (intimidate). Having studied their behavior over many years, I don't see abrasive bosses as bastards and bitches armed with sadistic motives. I've listened to them and put myself in their shoes, and through the process of empathy, I've discovered that they are fraught with the fear of incompetence—the terror of being perceived as inadequate, as failures. Furthermore, I believe that they defend against this unconscious fear with abrasive behaviors designed to protect their self-perception of supercompetence. This may explain why abrasive bosses do what they do, but it doesn't reveal the ori-gins of their behavior—where their distinctive behavioral style comes from. Why are some bosses adequate and others abrasive? Where did abrasive bosses learn to manage by aggression instead of affiliation? Who taught them that intimidation, rather than respect, is the preferable mode of motivation? And why are they driven to dominate—where did they learn that supercompetence is their only guarantee of survival?

5

On the Origins of Abrasion

Why They Do It

Abrasive bosses rely on aggression and domination to survive professionally and psychologically. They believe that intimidating coworkers into competence (by making you pay if you get in their way) ensures the preservation of their dominant status. This leads us to the inevitable question: why don't all bosses respond to incompetence with abrasive behavior? The answer is simple: *not all bosses are personally threatened by incompetence.* True, if your employees don't function adequately, that could threaten your production, but if you're an adequate boss, it won't threaten you personally. It won't change how you see yourself—it won't alter your self-image as a competent (good enough) boss. Adequate bosses don't experience employee incompetence as a psychological threat; they experience it as a problem to be solved. They look at each problematic situation objectively, and if it is determined to be the result of incompetence, they diagnose the cause(s) and address the situation in a civilized manner.

Identifying Incompetence: Ducks Versus Quacks

When confronted with a situation that suggests incompetence, adequate bosses shift into a simple diagnostic process, beginning with the obvious question: Is this in fact a case of incompetence? Did things screw up because of somebody's failure to function adequately or for some other reason(s)? Just because something quacks like a duck doesn't mean it's a duck. Adequate bosses research this very important question by taking the time to investigate. Whenever they get wind of a circumstance suggesting incompetence, they'll get off their chairs or on the phone and investigate further. Abrasive bosses, in contrast, are notorious for overreaction—leaping to assumptions and then catapulting to conclusions. For example, a friend of mine had worked at a company for many years when a new manager was assigned to her department. The manager asked my friend (who had a long track record of superior performance) to prescreen candidates for an open position. In the course of one screening interview, the candidate spontaneously volunteered that he was currently making x dollars and would not consider a lesser amount. My friend made no comment, as she understood that it was not her role to discuss salary issues. Following the interview, she sent an e-mail to her boss summarizing the interview and noted the candidate's comment about not considering less than x dollars. Seconds later her boss came flying out of his office in full attack mode, hackles raised: "Don't you know that it's totally inappropriate to discuss salaries with candidates—that's my job!"

Abrasive bosses will pounce on anything that suggests the slightest scent of incompetence. Adequate bosses, in contrast, don't leap to conclusions. Instead, they ask questions. My friend's boss could have asked a few polite questions to determine what exactly was said, thereby eliminating the risk of unjustly convicting a competent employee of incompetence. Instead, he immediately leapt to the conclusion that she was at fault—that she was incompetent. His chronic overreactions produced a painful pile of assumptions that were not only inaccurate—they were demoralizing. Over time my friend began to question her own competence, much as a battered spouse comes to wonder, "Maybe I did something to cause the problem—maybe it *was* my fault." His domineering, intimidating behavior achieved its aim: *it shook her up* and *put her down*. Unbeknownst to the boss, it also alienated her—she hit the trail in search of happier hunting grounds.

Differential Diagnosis and Treatment of Incompetence: The Adequate Boss Approach

If, upon examination, that which quacks like a duck is in fact a duck, the adequate boss will proceed to the next diagnostic step: determining the cause of incompetence. No self-respecting physician would blindly treat physical problems without first determining their cause, and the same holds for adequate bosses dealing with performance problems. And there's good news—it doesn't take years of training to master differential diagnosis of workplace incompetence. That's because there are only two—that's right, *two*—causes of workplace incompetence. Employees perform incompetently either because they *can't* do their work or because they *won't* do their work. They're either *unable* or *unwilling*. To determine the root cause of incompetence, adequate bosses take a systematic diagnostic approach, first considering the four reasons why people are *unable* to perform assigned tasks:

1. They lack the physical or mental ability.
2. They don't know what to do.
3. They don't know how to do it.
4. They lack the necessary resources.

People are unable to perform work competently when any one of these four conditions is present, namely, impairment, unclear expectations, inadequate training, or insufficient resources. And if a company has employees whose incompetence stems from any of these conditions, *it's the fault of the company, not the employee*. Think about it: it's a company's responsibility to adequately screen candidates to ensure that they have the physical, mental, and educational attributes required for a given position. Companies are also responsible for setting clear expectations (so that employees know *what* to do), providing company-specific training (so that they know *how* to do it), and supplying the necessary human or material resources to do the job.

If adequate bosses determine that incompetence results from inability, they quickly take responsibility for treating the root cause with clarified expectations, adequate training or resources, or humane accommodation or termination of the impaired employee.

If, after careful examination, adequate bosses rule out all these ability-related conditions, they then follow the other branch of this diagnostic decision tree: some employees perform incompetently not because they can't, but because they won't—*they're unwilling*. And why are employees unwilling to perform at a competent level? The reasons are endless: they may not like their work, their pay, their coworkers, their schedule, their boss, their working conditions, their commute, their position, their life, and so on, ad infinitum. They could perform competently, but they don't want to—they aren't motivated. Which leads us to our next question: should adequate bosses attempt to root out and cure these root causes of unwillingness?

Not necessarily—remember, we're talking about *adequate* bosses, bosses who are generally perceived to have *good enough*, if not great, management skills. At the very minimum they do an acceptable job of accommodating employee needs within organizational constraints. They are responsible for providing a respectful work environment, but they're not required to guarantee that we'll find our coworkers likeable or feel perfectly satisfied with our work schedules or office locations. Adequate bosses will accommodate individual need within reason, but not to the point of compromising the company's ability to function effectively. An adequate boss may allow a far-flung employee to telecommute (potentially boosting motivation) but only if telecommuting doesn't impair organizational performance.

Once adequate bosses conclude their diagnostic workups and treat the cause(s) of incompetence, as appropriate, they've fulfilled their responsibility. You've heard the old horse whisperer aphorism: "You can lead a horse to water, but you can't make it drink." Adequate bosses understand that this also applies to employees: you can provide sufficient support, direction, and respect, but once you've done that, you can't *make* an employee perform competently—that's his or her choice. And if, despite an adequate work environment, the employee chooses not to change, choosing instead to continue to perform below expectations, organizations have evolved a defense mechanism to unselect the unfit: the disciplinary process. Employees whose deficient performance jeopardizes the fitness of their company are, in Darwinian terms, threatened with organizational extinction. Through the disciplinary process they're advised of their maladaptive work behaviors and given an opportunity to adapt, survive, and hopefully thrive. Adequate bosses sit down with employees who have been deemed unfit, to calmly address the issue:

> "Andrew, you've worked for me for eight months. I've been very clear on my expectations, and it's clear to me that you have the experience and intelligence to do this job. You've been provided with the resources you need, and your performance is still not up to par. You're consistently late on your assignments, and the last project contained serious errors. I've been here to discuss any problems that come up, and I'm still not seeing acceptable results. I believe I've done all I can do—now it's up to you to meet expectations. I need to let you know that if these problems cannot be resolved, I'll have to take further action."

Adequate bosses handle this first step of the disciplinary process, the verbal warning, in an objective, respectful manner. Having confirmed the diagnosis of employee-based incompetence, they proceed through the standard steps of discipline:

1. Describe specific performance problem(s).
2. Clarify expectations for competent performance.

3. Determine if performance has sufficiently improved.

4. If so, apply positive reinforcement (carrot).

5. If not, apply consequences (disciplinary action).

Pretty basic stuff—you've heard it before if you were lucky enough to be given any supervisory training. By the way, this same discipline process is often recommended for kids, however without the standard workplace language recommending disciplinary action "up to and including termination." With the pipsqueak population, dessert deprivation and time-outs are better ways to go.

The Abrasive Boss Approach

Abrasive bosses treat incompetence very differently. They don't waste time researching underlying causes because if you're supercompetent you don't have to do any research—*you already know everything there is to know about incompetence.* You know that employees perform incompetently because they can't or won't do their work—they're unable or unwilling. And you know that they're unable because they're *stupid* and they're unwilling because they're either *lazy* or *stubborn*. Nothing complex here—people don't do what they're supposed to do the way they're supposed to do it because they are, in the words of abrasive bosses, loafers, idiots, or troublemakers. Because all these conditions are the fault of employees, it's up to the employees to fix them: the abrasive boss bears no responsibility. And if employees don't fix themselves, abrasive bosses swiftly apply their treatment for sloth, stupidity, and stubbornness: *aggression.*

> "I can't stand it when employees dumb down and projects fail. It kills me when they slack."

"I don't see how you treat nonperformers with respect and dignity. It's the driver in me—the job to get done is business."

"I don't have time to be nice—nasty is faster."

My favorite example of this mentality is the abrasive boss who was counseled by his human resource specialist to contain his aggression because he "would catch more flies with honey." His retort: *"Yeah, but you can attack more flies with shit!"*

Here's a summary of the diagnostic and treatment protocols used by abrasive bosses:

1. *See* incompetence (etiology: indolence, idiocy, insolence)
2. *Attack* incompetence (treatment: domination through intimidation)

Beware: for abrasive bosses, *perceived incompetence and actual incompetence are one and the same.* You don't have to *be* incompetent to be *perceived* as incompetent. Because, in their view, all human-related problems at work are the result of dozing, dullness, or defiance, there's no need to examine the organization's possible contributions to the problem. Nope—incompetence can only be caused by flawed employee character. And if you're in any way related to a problem at work, consider yourself a sitting duck. Remember, if something looks like incompetence or quacks like incompetence, abrasive bosses will *attack the duck*, thereby converting sitting ducks into dead ducks. As one coworker said of an abrasive boss:

"He tends to judge people and situations immediately—on his very first impression. He doesn't talk to them, doesn't explore the situation. He throws people in the trash heap. It could happen at any level. They feel the pressure.... They feel that he doesn't have faith in them.... It shakes them up and they make more mistakes."

This approach is deeply demoralizing to workers who take pride in their proficiency and then fall under the supervision of an abrasive boss. Too often I have observed the distress of capable employees who, despite their best efforts to demonstrate their ability and motivation, are unable to assuage their boss's unbridled anxiety over competence. It's much like the distress of faithful spouses who are continually accused of adultery—no matter how hard they try, they can never convince the accuser of their commitment. There's another parallel here, for many spouses who are continually accused of marital incompetence *actually begin to believe it.* They begin to question their own role: What did I do to deserve this? Did I do something wrong? You'll see the same phenomenon in employees constantly under suspicion of incompetence: they start to question themselves—they begin to have doubts about their own abilities. This anxiety over incompetence is contagious, transmitted from abrasive boss to distressed employee: "He thinks I don't know what I'm doing" is replaced by, "Maybe I *don't* know what I'm doing," which mutates into, "I don't know what I'm doing—*I must be incompetent.*" It's sad to see and sadder to experience.

The Evolution of Abrasion: A Case Study

Adequate bosses rely on civilized management and disciplinary processes to defend against threats to organizational competence. Abrasive bosses, however, are horses of a different color—they reflexively resort to overcontrol, threats, public humiliation, condescension, and overreaction to battle threats to their own competence. These distinctive threat displays serve to *shake people up* (intimidate) and *put people down* (dominate). Despite these behaviors, I don't see abrasive bosses as evil bastards and bitches, armed with diabolical motives. I don't believe they wake up every morning gleefully concocting fresh ways to torture their coworkers. Such behavior fits the description of the aberrant boss (sociopathic type).

If you ask horse whisperers why horses display aggression, they'll tell you it's not because horses are evil but because they fear a threat. Abrasive bosses aren't evil—*they're afraid.* I've listened to them and put myself in their shoes, and through this process of empathy I've discovered that they are driven by their unconscious fears of incompetence, their terror of being perceived to be inadequate—a failure. This may explain why abrasive bosses resort to aggression, but it doesn't reveal the origins of their behavior, the genesis of abrasion. Where did abrasive bosses learn to manage through aggression instead of affiliation? Who taught them that intimidation, rather than respect, is the preferable mode of motivation? And why are they driven to dominate? Who taught them that supercompetence is their only guarantee of survival?

Let's get the answers to these questions straight from the boss's mouth. Remember Mark (described in Chapter Three), armed with his "bazooka" strategies designed to "blast" coworkers into competence? On first acquaintance with Mark, the bastard diagnosis is understandable—he did bad things to good people for no apparent reason. I've shared my theory on why he and other abrasive bosses use aggression: they arm themselves with abrasive behaviors that defend against the threat of incompetence and, further, against unconscious fears of psychological annihilation and abandonment. Mark described his greatest fear: "the fear of failure, [of being] revealed to be a fraud, that I am incapable of doing what I've been given ... fearful of being destitute." To discover where Mark learned to fear incompetence and how he learned about aggression, I am going to ask you to step into the process of empathy. I'm going to ask you to step into Mark's shoes as he recounted his reaction to his own son's age-appropriate incompetence:

> "I realize I am heavily influenced by fear. I was creating
> that same fearful environment with [my team], but also
> with my kids. My son ... spilled a big bin of crayons.
> He spilled them and was terrified that I was [angry]....
> I have really let fear instill itself in my kid's life.... I
> didn't get mad [this time]. He couldn't find his shoes;
> [I told him to] go down and find them. I came down-
> stairs and he had the whole shoe basket, and I could
> tell he was really nervous.... This physical ability to
> turn myself into Darth Vader, to intimidate,... it makes
> me nervous."

Mark reflected on the origins of his anxiety in his fourth coaching session:

> "I don't feel like I've gotten the fear thing unwound.
> There is some deep-seated, painful childhood stuff."

He then went on to describe an early work situation where he was given unclear expectations and deprived of the resources to fulfill those expectations:

> "I hate it when people don't tell you what they want. I
> couldn't control everything.... That is a theme that
> did violence to my disposition ... given a reasonable,
> doable demand.... You aren't giving me any input,
> any control. Don't ever put me in a position where
> I can fail. I have to be successful. [If] I can't control
> the parameters, it would be worse for me to have my
> name on it, muck it up."

Barely pausing for breath, Mark proceeded to describe a terrifying childhood. He talked of his biological father "who beat [his mother] brutally" and whom she divorced when Mark was in kindergarten. Mark, his younger sister, and his mother then went to live with his maternal grandmother, "who threw us out—couldn't handle us after a year." Once they found housing, his mother was rarely home as she worked the graveyard shift to support her family:

> "I remember explicitly: when she woke up at 4:00 in the afternoon, one of the things I could do was make dinner. I was in second grade.... I had become used to being the man of the house. I was a barbequing second grader.... I don't want to be in a position where I had to be right. I would screw it up. It wasn't good. I was made to fail.... Being a parent, I can empathize with how horrible her situation [was], but ... one of her coping mechanisms. ... She would lose it and threaten to send us to the evil, alcoholic dad. She would start packing her clothes.... *If something is going to be wrong, I don't want my name on it. If something is going to be right, I want my name on it"* [emphasis added].

A few years later, Mark's mother married a military man who was not physically violent, and the threats of abandonment subsided. Still, Mark said,

> "Every other week was your week to be in the doghouse. It doesn't matter what I do, I am in the doghouse. [She would lecture me] on being inconsiderate and disrespectful.... [My stepfather] chimed in. He deferred to her."

Reading his own emotions to understand his fears of being an incompetent manager, Mark developed searing insight into the origins of his anxieties over competence. The risks of failing in his adult role were enormous, learned from his horrific childhood experience of threats of abandonment from his mother and threats of annihilation at the hands of a violent, alcoholic father. His grandmother had abandoned his mother in her time of need, and his mother in turn would threaten to abandon her son, perhaps to defend against the pain of recognizing her own incompetence as a mother. Mark now realized that he was transferring his own childhood experience onto *his* child. He was terrorizing his son as his mother had terrorized him and as her husband and mother had battered and abandoned her:

> "Once my son spilled some water in my study, and it spilled on my computer. I was making breakfast. He freaked out; he said he was sorry. My instant reaction was to get mad at him, [but] I didn't freak out. Then he spilled his chocolate milk all over the place. This milk went everywhere. I lost it. He wasn't paying attention [and] I got mad. I [gave him] this look—a look that can incite terror. . . ."

Mark soon saw the connection between his son's terror over spilt milk and his subordinates' fear of his wrath. His childhood cage had been continually rattled through threats of abandonment, annihilation, and accusations of incompetence: "My mother was inconsistent and moody. . .spilling milk one day was OK, but the next day it meant getting the snot beat out of you." Mark suddenly expressed gratitude regarding his boss, an authority figure in his adult life who treated him with respect:

> "The thing that was the most epiphanal [was] realizing what a thin margin of error I had lived with [for] so long. When I was in second grade, and Mom woke up, and if you did something wrong, [there were] all these variables. . . . If they didn't go right, then you could be shipped off. . . . The thin margin. What it made me think about, in reflection, [here at work] with [my boss]

I have never gotten the snot beaten out of me. There was a penalty with [my boss], but there was no abuse. If I make a mistake, it is not going to be the end of the world. There is part of me that is motivated to be very good and excellent. I want the bad part to go away.... I have been blessed with this gift of leadership, I am going to pour all of my time and energy [and] focus on the things I have control over. It is really nice to let go of trying to control [things I don't have control over]."

The positive effects of Mark's executive insight into his abrasive behavior extended to the home front:

"Sunday it dawned on me—my son is no longer terrified. Whatever I am doing differently, the reaction is no longer fear. [Now] he has the confidence to pout—[and] then move to open rebellion."

Mark smiled in a relaxed fashion as he made this observation. His satisfaction over releasing his son from fear was evident: his son now lived in a world where it was safe to pout, rebel, make mistakes, and be human. Mark's coworkers experienced a similar shift in their workplace climate. Freed of his own fear of incompetence, Mark made it safe for himself and his subordinates to be less than supercompetent—to be *human*.

Not all abrasive bosses are as vocal or insightful as Mark. Because I'm not doing therapy with my coaching clients, I don't take a psychosocial history. I do ask about their work history, and if clients choose to volunteer information about their upbringing, I listen closely. Early on in his coaching process, another client spontaneously insisted that his childhood was free of abuse:

"I love my parents; my dad was my hero ... but there was not that much love in the family, [it was] not expressed in the family until I was in the [military]. I always had food, clothes, had a great childhood. [My] father was a very good provider, no abuse, so we can get that out of the way.... He worked all the time. The necessities of life were the most important thing."

Only as he began to reflect on his own management style did this abrasive boss voice connections with his childhood experience. Following an instance when he was unjustly accused of laziness by his own boss, he stated:

"It makes me feel bad to be treated like that.... My dad did that for years. [My parents] had stringent rules; you didn't break them.... [My father] would accuse me of not doing the job. I told him, 'This is what I do.' [My father said] 'That's not the way I do it.' ... [It was a life] of hard work and parents beating my ass."

I wasn't surprised to hear this—in fact I'd been waiting for it. I listen carefully to the language abrasive bosses use in describing their experience of conflict at work. This individual's expressions had consistently depicted direct physical attack: "slap," "kick," "stab," "strangle," "shoot," "cut your head off," "destroy," "crucify," "rip," "whip," "whipping boy." I couldn't help but suspect that he had learned this language in childhood.

The Lesson: Survival = Competence at Any Cost

I've described how abrasive bosses reflexively leap to the conclusion that all incompetence is the result of flawed character. I've also discussed how they defend against this threat of incompetence with aggression—attack strategies consisting of one or more of the Big Five: overcontrol, threats, public humiliation, condescension, and overreaction. All of these strategies serve to intimidate, thereby ensuring the abrasive boss's dominance and continued survival. It became clear to me that abrasive bosses do not engage in the empathic process. They don't see any need to read and accurately understand why their coworkers perform below standards because *they already know:* incompetence stems from laziness, stupidity, or defiance.

What are the origins of this empathic blindness? Why do abrasive bosses disregard empathy in favor of aggression? What kind of answer do you expect if you ask a psychoanalytically oriented psychotherapist? You guessed it: *this behavior comes from their past—they learned it from someone.* Abrasive behavior, like other behavior, is learned through experience and experimentation. We may arrive in this world endowed with some basic instinct-driven behaviors (suck to get food, bawl to get burped, and so forth), but we humans don't spring from the womb fully equipped with well-defined strategies to intimidate and dominate. Some of us may have stronger genetic tendencies toward aggression, but I have yet to encounter an infant who reflexively accuses Mom of incompetence every time she's a few minutes late with the breast or bottle.

Animals learn to survive from their parents: their parents teach them how to read their environment and communicate in order to successfully feed, reproduce, and defend themselves. Charles Darwin (1872/1965) was the first to describe emotional communication in animals, analyzing the expression and reception of emotions in dogs, cats, monkeys, and diverse human groups. He concluded that the primary purpose of emotional expression was to create and maintain social order—to understand who's the boss or how to become one. James Gibson (1979) went on to describe the survival value of reading others' emotions:

Any animal needs to distinguish not only the substances and objects of the material environment, but also other animals and the differences between them. It cannot afford to confuse prey and predator, own-species with another species, or male with female [p. 7].

Other animals afford, above all, a rich and complex set of interactions, sexual, predatory, nurturing, fighting, playing, cooperating and communicating.... Each of these interactions requires the ability to convey and decipher emotional communication, to pay the closest attention to the optical and acoustic information that specifies what the other person is, invites, threatens and does [p. 128].

In other words, if social organisms want to survive, they have to learn how to read and interact with their environment in ways that promote survival. So if we've learned that aggression is the optimal mode of achieving our objectives, of securing our physical and psychological survival, who were our teachers? Let's start with the first organization we ever joined: the family. Our tutors could have been parents and other family members, or we could have learned how to treat others from religious, academic, and sports educators in our communities. We could also have learned about the survival value of abrasive behavior from superior officers in the military or our bosses at work. Wherever we got our education in abrasion, it contained five important lessons:

1. Survival requires competence.
2. Competence must be pursued at any interpersonal cost.
3. Threats to competence must be defended against at any interpersonal cost.
4. Intimidation promotes dominance.
5. Dominance assures survival.

If you ask abrasive bosses where they learned their management skills, many will tell you that they were "raised this way." But they'll rarely tell you that they suffered emotional abuse or neglect, because they don't see it or, unconsciously, they don't want to see it. They'll tell you that they grew up in families where hard work and achievement were highly valued—where parents

took a no-nonsense approach to child-rearing, demanding obedience and rewarding excellence. Many abrasive bosses see it as
an effective training ground for superior achievement, so the ends
justify the means: "I was raised this way and it worked for me;
look where it's gotten me."

In her book *For Your Own Good: Hidden Cruelty in Child-
Rearing and the Roots of Violence*, Alice Miller (1983) termed this
competence-oriented style of child-rearing *poisonous pedagogy*:

> Almost everywhere we find the effort, marked by varying degrees
> of intensity and by the use of various coercive measures, to
> rid ourselves as quickly as possible of the child within us—i.e.,
> the weak, helpless, dependent creature—in order to become an
> independent, competent adult deserving of respect. When we
> reencounter this creature in our children, we persecute it with the
> same measures once used on ourselves. And this is what we are
> accustomed to call "child-rearing" . . . [p. 58].

> [Poisonous pedagogy teaches] us that

> 1. Adults are the masters (not the servants!) of the dependent
>   child.
> 2. They determine in godlike fashion what is right and wrong.
> 3. The child is held responsible for their anger [p. 59].

Miller then describes the methods used in poisonous pedagogy:

> The methods that can be used to suppress vital spontaneity in the
> child are: laying traps, lying, duplicity, subterfuge, manipulation,
> "scare" tactics, withdrawal of love, isolation, distrust, humiliating
> and disgracing the child, scorn, ridicule and coercion even to the
> point of torture.

> It is also a part of "poisonous pedagogy" to impart to the child
> from the beginning false information and beliefs that have been

passed on from generation to generation and dutifully accepted by the young even though they are not only unproven but are demonstrably false [p. 59].

Miller lists these beliefs:

Parents deserve respect simply because they are parents.... Children are undeserving of respect simply because they are children.... Obedience makes a child strong.... Tenderness ... is harmful.... Responding to a child's needs is wrong.... Severity and coldness are a good preparation for life.... Parents are always right [p. 60].

Sound familiar? Here's how they translate into the abrasive workplace:

Bosses deserve respect simply because they are bosses.... Subordinates are undeserving of respect because they are subordinates.... Obedience makes a subordinate strong.... Bosses are always right.

I'm not the only one to suggest that abrasive bosses learned abrasion in their early years. The very limited research on managerial styles suggests a possible connection between past childhood abuse and workplace behavior (Bureau of National Affairs, 1990), with one study reporting that over 50 percent of executives exhibiting abrasive behavior reported experiencing childhood abuse (Henderson-Loney, 1996). At the same time, I don't believe that every child raised in an emotionally harsh environment is condemned to develop an abrasive work style: the ways in which humans shape their own futures are many and mysterious.

Abuse may not be the only factor involved: neglect of a child's emotions can also contribute to abrasive managerial behaviors in adulthood. For some abrasive bosses, emotions played a secondary role in their childhoods, expressed in statements such as, "We didn't talk about feelings in our family," or, "My father didn't show much emotion, unless he was upset about something." Such discouragement of emotional expression, especially of positive feelings, indicates that opportunities to feel *good enough* were severely limited or nonexistent in these families. The abrasive bosses I work with are constantly defending against the threat of being perceived as inadequate, incompetent, or in other words, *not good enough.* Those of us lucky enough to have been reared by emotionally attentive parents have a greater chance of developing stable self-esteem. Those of us unfortunate enough to be reared in families where emotions were neglected or abused are more vulnerable to developing insecurities about competence in our personal or professional lives. I believe that the greatest gift a parent can give a child is faith in that child's competence. My parents continually expressed their faith in me. I remember calling them from college, panicked that I wouldn't perform adequately on the next test or paper. And I also remember my parents' invariable response. "Calm down. You've got what it takes—you can do it." They were damn good kid whisperers.

Here's another observation: I've discovered that the later individuals are exposed to abrasion, the easier it is to rehabilitate their management styles. I've encountered a number of bosses who had fairly tranquil childhoods but in their first work experiences were exposed to highly abrasive work cultures. They naively concluded that the kick-ass management styles they were observing were not only acceptable but expected. Once they were made aware of the interpersonal wounds they'd inflicted, they readily abandoned their (as one client framed it) "Neanderthal" management styles in favor of the more positive approaches they had experienced in childhood. Competence anxiety isn't deeply ingrained in these individuals—it's not hard for them to change.

Contrast this with the abrasive boss I quoted earlier who said, "I don't see how you treat nonperformers with respect and dignity." He meant it in all sincerity, and I know this because he's the same boss who suffered his father's continual accusations of incompetence, the same boss who described his childhood as a life "of hard work and parents beating my ass." He truly couldn't see how treating incompetence with respect and dignity could ever yield results because *he'd never experienced such treatment.* He treated his coworkers as he had been treated—as a lazy, stupid, disobedient kid who could only be motivated into competence with aggression. Some abrasive bosses don't know any better *because they were never treated any better.*

I hold that the character of a family is predicated on the character of the parents. I also believe that the character of a company is predicated on the character of its leaders. Adequate bosses create emotionally adequate, humane environments characterized by respect—they diagnose and remedy work problems without doing interpersonal damage. Abrasive bosses are horses of a very different color—they lack the empathic ability to read and understand the many possible reasons for incompetence, lunging instead to accuse and convict. And because they don't read people, they have little or no insight into how to build internal motivation and commitment. Earlier I noted that you can motivate a horse with carrots or sticks. Positive rewards build motivation—wild horses may show up every day for a carrot—but horse whisperers will tell you that they won't show up every day for a beating. Domesticated horses, children, and employees all have one thing in common: they're tied by the ropes of dependency. They depend on their owners, parents, and bosses for food, shelter, protection, and, they hope, emotional sustenance. If they're harnessed to someone who wields psychological sticks instead of carrots, there's no easy escape. Why don't abrasive bosses see the negative consequences of flogging? Why don't they see the damage they do to coworkers and, ultimately, to themselves? They don't see the wounds because they're blind to emotion—blinder than bats.

6

Blinder Than Bats

Why They Don't See

I once met with the head of a hospital human resource division who was interested in referring a medical director for coaching. He described the individual as an intelligent man with a management style characterized by threats, overreaction, and overcontrol. Then he paused, musing: "Here's what I don't understand. When I brought these issues to his attention, he was totally surprised. He had no idea that his words and actions caused such offense. And in the next breath he insisted that his behavior wasn't an issue, contending that his employees were just being overly sensitive." The HR head paused again and then turned to me: "I don't understand—why don't they see what they do? And when you point it out to them, why don't they get that they're hurting others—that they're doing damage?" This question was followed with a refrain I hear over and over again: "*They just don't see—they just don't get it.*"

Contrary to the popular belief that abrasive bosses carefully concoct elaborate management strategies designed to destroy their coworkers, I have found the exact opposite to be the case. Abrasive bosses generally don't see the impact of their behavior on coworkers, and if they do, they don't get the fact that they are causing significant emotional harm. Bluntly speaking, they are blind or ignorant or both. They just don't see—they just don't get it. When it comes to emotions, abrasive bosses are blinder than bats.

I say *blinder* than bats, because bats can see when we can't. They've got little eyeballs that function well during the day but are useless at night without light. However, when they can't see with their eyes, they use their ears. Bats can navigate and avoid collisions with other bats through *echolocation*, a sensory sonar system used to detect prey and obstacles. They emit high-pitched sounds that bounce off objects, creating an echo, which they then read to prevent run-ins with fellow bats. Through this highly accurate process of echolocation, bats "see" with their ears, avoiding collisions with other objects. Abrasive bosses are blinder than bats—they lack an *emotionlocation* system. They have little or no ability to detect others' emotions, and as a result they are unable to avoid damaging run-ins with coworkers. And when their offending words or actions make contact, more often than not they don't see the emotional impact craters that result. Unable to see their effect on others, they persist in flying blind—rubbing people raw through continual interpersonal collisions. In summary:

- They don't see their impact on others and therefore don't understand that the impact is injurious (they're blind *and* ignorant).
  or
- They see some impact, but they have no idea of the nature or degree of pain they've inflicted (they're not blind, but they're ignorant).

The first condition is the more common: many abrasive bosses don't see that their behavior has any impact on coworkers' emotions. They don't see that their behavior is in any way related to how others respond to their management directives. They don't see, and thus they don't understand—blindness blocks insight. Let me offer a classic example. During a coaching session a CEO complained to me that his senior management team sat silently when he pressed them for ideas or reactions. When I asked why he thought they didn't respond, he answered: "I don't know—they're either lazy or stupid." True to form, he reflexively rendered the abrasive boss diagnosis of incompetence. In his eyes, they didn't speak up because they were indolent or intellectually impaired. He was totally blind to the possibility (later confirmed as fact) that his management team didn't voice their ideas for fear of being attacked by the CEO. He didn't see that his past attack behaviors influenced his team's emotions, instilling fear. Unable to see his effect on his team, he had no possibility of comprehending the crushing effects of his intimidating style on team communication.

Let's consider the second condition: ignorance, or *sight without insight*. Here, abrasive bosses see some impact from their behavior, but they have no idea of the nature or degree of the pain they've inflicted. I once worked with a plant manager who openly admitted that he yelled at his subordinates to "get them off their asses." He added: "They're used to it—they know how I am. They'll get pissed for a minute, but they don't take it seriously." This boss had yet to learn that he was referred for coaching after his company's human resource specialist overheard members of his team angrily joking that someone needed to "put a contract out on his head." Upon further excavation, the specialist discovered a deep crater of employee resentment, while the boss remained ignorant of the extreme alienation induced by his abrasive behavior.

Social Sonar

Much like the hospital HR executive mentioned earlier, most people are mystified as to why abrasive bosses can't see their destructive effect on others. I struggled with these same questions when I first started coaching: Why didn't these oftentimes intellectually gifted people see what they did to others? Where was their social sonar? Why didn't they "get it"? As I pondered these questions, it dawned on me that I suffered from the opposite condition—an *overly* sensitive emotional sonar system. As a kid I kept hearing that I was "too sensitive," and was frequently advised to "not let things bother you so much." Looking back, I realize that I was constantly monitoring my childhood world for subtle changes in emotional climate and was deeply affected by the slightest suggestion of suffering in others. I also realize that the admonitions to toughen up were made not in reproach but because loved ones didn't want me to suffer. They felt that if I were less sensitive—less aware of emotion—I would then be less vulnerable to the pain that life inevitably inflicts. At the same time, I always viewed my hypersensitivity to others' emotions as a failing—a shortcoming—like being too slow or too messy or, in my case, too sensitive. Only later in life did I realize that my finely tuned emotional sonar would be of great benefit in my earlier careers of psychotherapist and executive, and later as a boss whisperer. This overdeveloped emotionlocation system amplified my empathic abilities. I was endowed with a level of supercompetence when it came to developing insight.

Abrasive bosses lack this emotional sonar, or their reception is faulty, picking up only a few feedback transmissions that are either ignored or not taken seriously. The result: abrasive bosses remain blind to their impact on others, or when they do see it, they discount or deny the resulting wounds. In his book *Working with Emotional Intelligence*, Daniel Goleman (1998) eloquently defines emotional intelligence as the ability to *read* and *manage* one's own and others' emotions "so that they are expressed appropriately and effectively, enabling people to work together smoothly toward their common goals" (p. 7). Abrasive bosses may possess exceptional cognitive intelligence, but they are dramatically deficient in emotional intelligence. Abrasive bosses generally don't read emotions, and on the rare occasions that they do, they inevitably underestimate their significance.

Why don't abrasive bosses see what they do? Why don't they seem to care? I didn't have any answers to these questions when I started out as a coach, but I came across some clues in my clients' reactions to coworker feedback. More often than not these bosses were blindsided by the nature and degree of the distress voiced by their subordinates, peers, and superiors—they were *shocked*. Their responses revealed their lack of insight into their continual collisions with coworkers. Those who hadn't seen their impact on others (the blind) would characteristically express their astonishment as follows:

"I can't believe that they took me seriously."

"Do I really have that effect on people?"

"I'm shocked that they see me this way."

"What are they all worked up about? I don't get it."

Those who had detected some impact but had no concept of the magnitude of the blows (the ignorant) would portray others' pain as unreasonable or unjustified:

"They're making a mountain out of a molehill—a big deal out of nothing."

"Just because I don't treat them with kid gloves—how could they think I'm out to get them?"

"I don't see why they're so angry. They should realize that when I get on their case it's nothing personal. It's just business—the job has to get done."

My observations corresponded with research that indicates that most people who inflict distress do not intend to hurt others. In one study, over 80 percent of perpetrators indicated that they had no intention of hurting others' feelings (Leary, Springer, Negel, Ansell, & Evans, 1998). Additional studies have found that people engage in abrasive behaviors *out of sheer ignorance*, lacking awareness of the appropriate interpersonal rules (Metts, 1994), or because they have some type of social skill deficit (Miller, 2001).

One afternoon many years ago I was sitting with a client who was in the throes of shock and confusion over his feedback.

His reactions stirred in me the same questions voiced by the HR executive: Why don't they see what they do? Why don't they care? *Why don't they get it?* I was suddenly jolted in my chair by an enlightening bolt of insight: you *can't* care about something *you don't see* and *don't understand*. Eureka! Maybe abrasive bosses didn't seem to care because they were sightless and thus incapable of insight. This blinder-than-bats hypothesis flew in the face of all the bully experts who insisted that abrasive behavior stems from diabolical intent. What if abrasive bosses *weren't* bats out of hell? What if they were blinder than bats, unable to detect and decipher emotions? And if they were blind, why were they blind? Were they somewhere else when the empathy genes were handed out, or were their parents somewhere else when it came time to teach these kids how to read and accurately interpret emotions?

Accurate Empathy

To answer this question of nature versus nurture, I roamed the research on empathy and made a heartening discovery: *empathy is learned*. But before we go any further, I want to revisit this process of reading emotions in more detail. Translated from its Greek roots, *empathy* means *feeling with*, or *feeling into*. Empathy *doesn't* mean sympathy. People often confuse the two, but sympathy means *feeling for*—when your house burns down, I feel sorry *for* you. Empathy means *feeling with*—when your house burns down I try to feel *with* you, and to do that I try to read what you're feeling by putting myself in your shoes (or in the case of horse whisperers, in the horse's hooves). Despite the common usage of the term, empathy isn't something you *have*; it's something you *do* to decipher how others are feeling. You see behavior (dog wagging tail) and then strive to read its meaning (welcome?). Reading emotion is like reading a word. It's not enough to simply see the letters B-A-T; you must also accurately interpret their meaning to determine whether the writer is referring to a form taken by vampires or an instrument of baseball. Researcher William

Ickes (1997) terms this *empathic accuracy: seeing* the behavioral expression of emotion and *getting it,* accurately understanding the meaning of the moment.

Believe it not, animals depend on empathic accuracy to survive. We've already talked about the fact that awareness of one's environment is essential if you want to deduce who's the biggest boss and the foxiest fox and where to find the five-star shelter and premier prime rib dinner. We've also examined the child-rearing practices that teach baby bosslets that aggression is the preferred defense against threats to professional survival. Despite this training, abrasive bosses are blind to the importance of others' emotions—they're burdened with a blind spot of (woolly) mammoth proportions. If you can't read emotions, you're doomed to extinction—woe to the marmot who reads a grizzly's grimace as an expression of affiliative rather than annihilative intent.

Animals learn to read emotions accurately because the price of inaccurate empathy could be one's life. In this process of emotional communication they send and receive signals to determine if it's better to fight, flee, or fraternize. So if birds and bees and bears and bats do it, why don't abrasive bosses use empathy to read how their coworkers feel in response to their wounding words and actions? It's simple—*they never learned how.* Amazingly, empathy is learned. And where do animals, human and otherwise, learn it from? You guessed it—*from each other.* When immature animals are deprived of contact with other members of their species (rendering them *social isolates*), they end up emotionally blinder than bats. They never learn how to emit, much less read, species-specific emotional communications. Research on a wide variety of species, including dogs, wolves, monkeys, chimpanzees, and humans, has shown early social deprivation to be associated with serious deficits in later social competence (Buck & Ginsburg, 1997). Studies of maternally deprived rhesus monkeys demonstrated that such deprivation resulted in severe social deficits in the infant animal. When these monkeys became mothers, they displayed no maternal bonding behavior—*no emotional communication* with their infants (Harlow & Suomi, 1970). These social isolates lack social sonar—they never learned how to send or receive species-specific emotional signals. In the course of these research ramblings, I read something else that blew me out of my boss-whisperer's saddle:

> Such creatures demonstrate species-typical displays; however, they do not use these displays appropriately when placed with other animals, nor do they appear accurately to "read" the displays of others. On the other hand, if these socially deprived individuals are given social experience—particularly that involving "behavior pacemakers" . . . the ability to communicate accurately is attained [Buck & Ginsburg, 1997, p. 29].

Do you know what that means? I'll tell you what it means—it means that *empathy can be learned*. And not only that—it means that empathy can be learned *later in life*. It means that if you put someone who hasn't learned empathy with someone who has (the behavior pacemaker, or coach), adults—and more specifically abrasive bosses—can learn to *see, understand,* and *care* about coworkers' emotions. I'd like to say that this insight revolutionized my coaching practice, but it didn't—I was already teaching empathy and didn't know it. I was already asking empathy-related questions of each of my clients: "How do you think your superiors (or peers or subordinates) feel when you say (or do) that?" or "How would you feel if *your* boss treated you that way?" Unbeknownst to me, I was engaged in the process of inducing empathy.

Perceptive Pedagogy and Empathic Adequacy

Recent research suggests that immature members of *Homo sapiens* learn to empathize through *parental induction*, an intervention empathically savvy parents use when they observe abrasive behavior in their young (Hoffman, 2000). Let's say that you've just socked your little sister in the head for taking your toy truck. Adequate parents will teach empathy by asking you to step into your sister's shoes: "You shouldn't hit your sister. See—you've made her cry. How do you think she feels? How do you think *you'd* feel if someone did that to you?!" To induce empathy, you (the aggressor) are first given feedback that your behavior has had an impact not just on your sister's head but on her emotions as well: "See—you've made her cry." You're then asked how you would feel if you were in your sister's shoes (or head): "How do you think she feels? How do you think you'd feel if someone did that to you?!" Those are the baby steps of empathy. Looking back I can see that my empathic training was enhanced by my family background: if you're born to a corn farmer, you grow up knowing a lot about corn, and if you're born to a psychiatrist, you grow up knowing a lot about emotions. This explained why my social sonar was always so sensitively attuned to the slightest changes in emotional climate.

Empathically adequate parents teach their children to read emotions so that they become skilled social communicators. From what my clients have revealed about their childhoods, I suspect they were reared by empathically inadequate parents—parents who hadn't been taught to read emotions by their own parents. I suspect that in these families, emotions were accorded minimal attention—they weren't important enough to discuss. And the emotions that were expressed focused on displays of aggression to "motivate" the child to fulfill the parental concept of competence.

So there you have it—my hypotheses of why abrasive bosses are blinder than bats, why they don't see the emotional impact they have on others—why they don't "get it." They didn't receive an adequate education in empathy—they weren't trained to see and read other people's emotions. And this blind spot makes it impossible to care, because you *can't* care about feelings you can't see, emotions that (to you) don't exist—sightlessness precludes insight. Now here's the million-dollar question: if abrasive bosses could learn to see what they do, would they begin to care enough to stop doing it? And here's my two cents' worth on that topic, based on years of coaching these individuals: *yes*. If these emotionally blind bosses can be made to see what they do, there's a very good chance that they'll begin to care enough to stop doing it. There's one hitch: they won't learn the empathic process willingly. They have to be *made* to see what they do. And to take their blinders off, you'll have to take the (forgive me this once) bull(y) by the horns.

7

Why We Don't Take Bulls (or Bosses) by the Horns

There's no question that abrasive bosses do harm. So why don't we confront them and put an end to the pain they cause? Why don't peers and subordinates stand up for themselves? Why don't superiors step in and set limits? Your local matador will tell you that stepping into the bullring to take a bull by the horns is extremely risky business. The same holds for abrasive bosses. People don't step in to confront abrasive bosses for the same reason that people (with the exception of a few very well paid matadors) don't take bulls by the horns—*they're afraid*. There it is again, that same threat → fear → defense dynamic that we examined in bears, bosses, and now coworkers. Abrasive bosses perceive coworker incompetence, which stirs anxiety over their own competence and survival, which in turn provokes the *fight* defense: aggression. In response to this aggressive threat, coworkers experience survival anxiety and resort to the *flight* defense: withdrawal, otherwise known as *lying low*. We don't take the problem of abrasive bosses by the horns because we're afraid of getting gored—psychologically and professionally.

The View from Below

It's no mystery why subordinates are afraid to confront an abrasive boss. Consider these synonyms for subordinate: *subservient, inferior, submissive*. As a subordinate you don't have authority over your boss—you're an underdog to the top dog. Powerlessness is a pretty poor starting point for setting limits with an abrasive boss, because if you challenge your boss's dominance, *the only way to go is down (or out)*. Subordinates in nonhuman dominance hierarchies quickly learn the dangers of challenging the leader, and it's no different for humans chained to the command of an abrasive boss. Confronted with a direct challenge to their authority, abrasive bosses defend their supremacy with retaliatory aggression. These aren't the nonlethal, day-to-day threat displays we've seen abrasive bosses (and alpha wolves) use to intimidate and thus motivate subordinates into compliance. No, direct challenges to dominance can provoke mortal combat in which aggression has a single, very dangerous objective: a fight to the death to eliminate the threat. In the animal kingdom elimination can be achieved through death, disabling injury, or exile. In the corporate kingdom these translate to termination, crippling devaluation, or relegation to the company's Timbuktu sales office.

They say elephants never forget—let me tell you, employees never forget the fate of coworkers who fought back against an abrasive boss. These duels to the death are branded into their psyches. Listen to a coworker describe an abrasive attorney's go-for-the-jugular response to one such dominance challenge:

> "She came flying out of her office and started yelling at Mara, our administrative assistant: 'What is wrong with you that you can't get me the files I asked for?! *What do I have to do to get you to do your job?!*" You could tell that Mara had had enough—she'd worked there for twenty years, and nobody ever treated her that way. She was literally trembling with anger, but she stood up for herself: 'The files won't be released from the court until next week. I already told you that—I sent you an e-mail yesterday. And I don't appreciate being attacked.' The attorney exploded: 'You can't talk to me that way! How dare you talk to me that way. I'm going to have you written up for insubordination!'"

It's an all-too-common tale, a three-act play of attack, defense, and death: (1) abrasive boss attacks subordinate; (2) subordinate defends self through fight rather than flight; (3) abrasive boss moves in for the kill. *The End.* These public executions are particularly instructive, allowing bystanders to observe coworkers sticking their necks out, only to have those necks end up on the chopping block. Fairy tales serve to teach children this same lesson, a lesson learned by Alice in the course of her adventures in Wonderland:

> [I]n a very short time the Queen was in a furious passion, and went stamping about, and shouting "Off with his head!" or "Off with her head!" about once in a minute.
>
> Alice began to feel very uneasy: to be sure, she had not as yet had any dispute with the Queen, but she knew that it might happen any minute, "and then," thought she, "what would become of me? They're dreadfully fond of beheading people here: the great wonder is, that there's any one left alive!" [Carroll, 1865/1941].

Annihilation isn't the only effective defense against subordinate uprisings—abandonment can work equally as well. In this strategy the abrasive boss abandons the offending employee, a tactic more commonly known as *writing them off* and *waiting them out.* As one abrasive boss confessed: "I do discard people—write them off, discard them. . . . I am very spontaneous when it comes to assessing somebody. I value some—I give them more time. The ones I don't value—I write them off."

In this approach the abrasive boss first determines that the offending individual is "difficult" and thus unworthy of the boss's time or attention:

> "If he isn't going to do his job, I'm not going to babysit him."
>
> "She's a total incompetent. Why should I waste my time on her?!"

"All he does is complain about problems. I'm not going to put up with it."

Starvation motivates animals to migrate in search of food; abrasive bosses apply this same principle to unwanted employees. Once employees have been written off as undeserving, it is simply a matter of time to wait them out:

"Once he figures out he's not going to be promoted, he'll be out of here."

"I don't want her here—it's only a matter of time until she leaves."

"One more incident and he's out."

Adequate bosses take the time to explore and thoughtfully address incompetence. As we've discussed, abrasive bosses don't have that kind of time: "I don't have time to be nice—nasty is faster." If investing one's time in aggression doesn't kill off these perceived "good-for-nothings," abandonment works almost as well—simply starve them of psychological and professional sustenance until they're forced to seek survival elsewhere.

The View from Above

There's no mystery about why subordinates fear to tread upon an abrasive boss's dominance. But what about the abrasive boss's superiors (here referred to as *management*)? What keeps management from handling abrasive bosses? What wild horses dragged management away from the task of setting limits on abrasive behavior that disrupts the smooth flow of operations? Don't these managers (including human resource staff) have the power to rein in this destructive aggression? Why don't they use it?

Here's the answer, straight from this boss whisperer's mouth: managers avoid handling the abrasive bosses who work under them because *they're afraid.* Yes, it's that same ol' threat → fear →

defense dynamic in yet another incarnation. And these managers harbor even more fears than subordinates or peers. Their fears fall into two categories: the fear of *being harmed* by the abrasive boss and the fear of *doing harm* to the abrasive boss. As I advised managers on the steps they'd need to take to rein in abrasive bosses, most of these seemingly decisive types would dig in their heels. I gained deeper insight into this phenomenon when I explored their fears in a group context. Years ago I was approached by a human resource specialist who was frustrated by the fact that her company's management avoided dealing with problem employees, including the abrasive bosses who reported to them. Her words to me were: "They just won't do it—they won't confront the individual until it's a crisis, and then they knock down my door trying to get *me* to deal with the situation. It's their job to manage their people—not mine. Could you provide a workshop that would train them to do it?"

I knew that if I trotted out the standard training approach (document carefully, provide feedback, set expectations, monitor for improvement), I'd be beating a dead horse. These managers didn't need training—they already knew *what* they were supposed to do. They needed management whispering—they needed to identify *why* they weren't doing it; they needed to develop insight into the fears that kept them from handling the abrasive bosses they were responsible for. To develop their executive insight, I applied the Socratic method by posing the following question: "Why don't managers confront an abrasive boss?" Note the phrasing—it would have been too threatening to ask why they were "afraid" to confront abrasive bosses, because fear is one of those taboo emotions at work, especially for management. Despite my careful third-person wording, these managers immediately responded in the first person, beginning with their fears of *doing harm* to the abrasive boss:

> "He's turned this place around financially—I don't want to get on his case."

"He's already got financial [or family or health] problems—
I don't want to add to his burden."

"What if she cries?" (A scenario dreaded by most male
managers.)

"I don't want to damage his morale—he's our lead man
on the new project."

"I don't want to hurt her feelings—she's been loyal to me
and works harder than anyone else."

"He's got some difficult people on his team—I don't want
to undermine him."

"I've worried that he could go off the deep end—that he
might kill himself."

Surprised by that last comment? I was too, and I remain
surprised at how often members of management voice fears that
the abrasive boss will become self-destructive if confronted on
his or her interpersonal incompetence. I believe these anxious managers unconsciously sense how closely the abrasive
boss's self-esteem is linked to his or her psychological survival.
They're frightened that they will upset this fragile balance if they
strip the abrasive boss of that all-important self-image of supercompetence. These fears of doing harm, once expressed, were
followed by fears of being harmed by the abrasive boss:

"If he got pissed off and quit, we'd be in deep doo-doo."

"Are you kidding? He's the last person I want angry at
me!"

"Chances are she'd accuse me of the same behaviors, and
I'm not perfect."

"Talking to him won't help—it'll just make things worse."

"If I bring it up, she'll take it out on the employees who
complained."

"If he quits, I'll just end up having to do his job on top of
mine."

"I don't know what he'd do—he's the type that could go postal."

I vividly recall one inexperienced management team that had been paralyzed by the threats of an abrasive middle manager. Her rough treatment of subordinates became evident soon after she was hired, and when her (male) manager addressed this in a reasonable manner, she cut him off, declaring she wouldn't tolerate being undermined by a "bunch of men." In the same breath she mentioned that she had sued a former employer for discriminatory practices. I arrived on the scene a few months later at the request of the corporate human resource department to assist with what HR staff termed "a communication problem."

The place was a mess. The abrasive boss was riding roughshod over her subordinates, and their cries of distress to the management team were met with silence. What was going on? Why weren't they handling the situation?! Repressing my impassioned gut reaction to this suffering, I instead deployed empathy to diagnose the underlying cause(s) of management's paralysis. As I talked with each member of the team in an attempt to put myself in their shoes, I discovered *they* were shaking in their shoes. One confessed his terror at the prospect of handling this abrasive boss: "I can't risk taking her on—I have kids to put through college and a mortgage to pay." For a moment I didn't understand what he was saying, but then it dawned on me that he was afraid of being personally sued. There it was again, the survival dynamic: threat (of suit) → fear (of financial annihilation) → defense (flight through avoidance). When they heeded my management whisperings and consulted their corporate legal department, they discovered (to their great relief) that they were indemnified from personal liability in carrying out their management duties. Only when they were freed from the threat of financial assault could they successfully set limits on the abrasive boss.

Management's Mechanisms of Defense

The Mystery of the Missing Managers was solved: superiors flee the task of handling abrasive bosses because they're afraid of doing harm *to* or being harmed *by* these aggressive individuals. And thanks to empathy, who can blame them? What managers in their right mind would want to throw themselves on the horns of this dilemma, only to risk being impaled? Faced with this threat, the superiors of abrasive bosses resort to *defense*, defined by biologists as any trait that reduces the likelihood that an organism (or part of an organism) will be consumed by a predator or wounded from attack (Cloudsley-Thompson, 1980). A biologist of the mind, Sigmund Freud viewed defenses similarly, referring to them as the "psychical correlative of the flight reflex" (1905/1960, p. 233). Like horses, bosses of abrasive bosses rely on flight, practically stampeding toward the door to avoid handling the threat of aggression. However, because they're paid to show up at work and can't physically flee the scene of abrasive bosses' interpersonal crimes, these managers run defense via three avoidance maneuvers: *denial*, *displacement*, and *delay*.

Denial

Denial is a handy-dandy defense mechanism. All you have to do is *deny the problem exists*. It's not hard to detect denial in managers of abrasive bosses. Listen in:

> "He's just got some difficult employees."
>
> "Her department is under a lot of pressure—things will improve."
>
> "He doesn't blow up that often."
>
> "He's not the first to lose it around here, and he won't be the last."

Each of the previous statements acknowledges the abrasive boss's behavior but at the same time denies the possibility that he or she has, or *is*, a problem:

"He's just got some difficult employees." (*He's not the problem—his employees are.*)

"Her department is under a lot of pressure—things will improve." (*She's not the problem—the pressure is the problem.*)

"He doesn't blow up that often." (*It doesn't happen often enough to be a problem.*)

"He's not the first to lose it around here, and he won't be the last." (*He's not the problem—we're the problem, and since we all do it, it's not a problem.*)

Denial allows us to shift the problem onto other people (in this case, employees) or phenomena ("a lot of pressure"). Denial also allows us to redefine the criteria for the problem. "He doesn't blow up that often" defines the problem as one of frequency versus force. I don't know about you, but I can't imagine an attorney defending a client against homicide charges by saying, "He doesn't shoot people often enough for it to be a problem." Denial also allows us to dilute the problem, by normalizing it as something we all do.

Displacement

Displacement is another popular flight strategy used by management to avoid intervening with an abrasive boss. More commonly referred to as the "head 'em up—move 'em out" strategy by horse whisperers, displacement of these unmanageable individuals can be achieved in a number of ways, including *transfer, isolation,* and *starvation.* Transfer (also known as the *geographic cure*) involves facilitating the transfer of an abrasive boss to another division or department, where he or she can inflict injury on entirely new (and usually unwitting) populations. I am continually amazed by seemingly ethical managers who, devoid of guilt, sing the praises of their about-to-depart abrasive boss to the unsuspecting new department: "He brings a lot to the table" (*yeah, right*). Isolation consists of removing the abrasive boss from any supervisory responsibilities and relegating the offender to a role that demands minimal interaction with coworkers (also known as *solitary confinement*). Starvation refers to the practice of eliminating an abrasive boss's sources of professional or psychological sustenance. This can be achieved by reassigning the boss to uninteresting, unrewarding, and conspicuously humiliating tasks in the hope of starving him or her out of the organization.

Delay

Delay is a less effective avoidance tactic because, unlike in denial, management is required to recognize that the abrasive boss is in fact a problem. But here's the great thing about this particular defensive maneuver: it allows management to conclude, "Yes, we have a problem, but *it just might go away if we avoid confronting it!*" For example:

> "We're hoping things will improve after he gets through this divorce."
>
> "We hear she might transfer to another division."
>
> "Things may look very different after the merger."
>
> "It won't be long before he retires."
>
> "It won't be long before I retire."

In its more extreme manifestation, delay takes the form of unrealistic, desperate fantasizing, also known as the *pray-for-a-miracle* approach. Such prayers can range from the innocuous ("maybe she'll marry the guy and decide to quit") to the malevolent ("please let him be hit by a beer truck"). Unlike denial, where we turn a blind eye to the problem, delay allows us to avoid handling the problem even though we see it. Unfortunately, delay is a time-limited defense strategy, as anyone who has lingered too long in the path of a bus will confirm.

Not all managers flee when faced with an abrasive boss: some take a stand and attempt to fight the problem by offering personal mentoring or referring the abrasive individual to a good executive coach. Others go with the more standard training options, ranging from generic leadership development approaches to anger management and team development seminars—all questionable as far as their effectiveness with abrasive bosses goes. When I surveyed *BusinessWeek*'s top-ranked U.S. executive education programs, none offered what one respondent referred to as "a charm school for assholes" (Crawshaw, 2005). In contrast, anger management courses for executives and physicians are proliferating, despite the lack of research to substantiate their effectiveness (Hollenhorst, 1998). And then there's the revered "positive" approach to preventing and healing further abrasion: the trust-building workshop.

(Dis)Trust Building

I have a deep distrust of trust-building workshops. I have never been able to buy into the concept that a single, consultant-driven intervention could transform an agitated herd of employees into a unified team ready to pull whatever wagon they're hitched to, much less tame an abrasive boss. My suspicions were confirmed when I was recruited into an executive position with a Fortune 100 company to run its national and international employee assistance programs. Acclimated to the spartan stratum of social work, I was thrilled to ascend to the glorious galaxy of corporate life, complete with national conventions at luxurious locales. My first experience in corporate team building took place at

San Diego's fabled Hotel del Coronado. After the obligatory welcome speeches, we were herded out onto the beach (the same beach strolled by Marilyn Monroe in *Some Like It Hot*) to build the bonds that bind.

These people were new to me—I'd never met any of them. Intent on conveying my newly minted corporate composure, I was careful not to betray my skepticism. I, along with my new comrades, listened attentively to the consultant's instructions: "I want everyone to stand in a circle, facing inward. And then one of you will stand in the middle of the circle, stiffen your body, and fall backward. This is a trust-building exercise: the objective is to trust your teammates to catch you as you fall."

We obediently formed our circle, and one woman of slight build volunteered to stand in the center. We braced to catch her. Facing me, she stiffened and fell back. And then it happened—I couldn't believe my eyes. The team members immediately behind her stiffened and stepped back. *Thwump!* She fell flat on her back, biting the proverbial dust (or in this case, sand). Silence prevailed—shocked looks were exchanged by all. Turning to the person on my left, I hissed, "*What the hell happened?*" His reply: "All I know is that no one likes her—she can be a real pain." My convictions regarding trust building were forever confirmed: trust can't be engineered—it has to be earned.

To Flee or Not to Flee

The same law holds for natural and corporate jungles: only the fittest survive. And to survive, inhabitants of these jungles operate according to the same survival dynamic: threat → fear → defense. This dynamic applies equally to abrasive bosses and to their subordinates, managers, and peers (I haven't commented separately on peers because I've found that they share management's same fears of doing harm to or being harmed by their abrasive colleagues). Each perceives threat, feels fear, and defends through fight or flight. As we've seen, abrasive bosses go for the fight option, battling threats to their competence. As their coworkers, you have the same options—to flee (or at least lie low) or to fight the threat of psychological and professional injury inflicted by abrasive bosses. Many of you have developed significant expertise in the flight options, or you wouldn't be reading this book. You also know that these options aren't terribly effective in defending against the unfriendly fire of workplace abrasion. Whether you're a subordinate, peer, or manager of an abrasive boss, if you want to stop the suffering you'll have to squelch your impulse to flee and, instead, take a stand with the strategies presented in the coming chapters. But before anyone can be persuaded to take a bull or boss by the horns, one question must be answered: Why bother? Why risk getting gored if there's no hope? Why bother to climb into the ring if, as one manager assured me, "They can't change"?

8

Can Bosses Change Their (Blind) Spots?

Whenever people hear that I coach abrasive bosses, I'm asked the same question over and over again: *Can leopards change their spots?* They're not really asking about leopards—they're challenging the possibility that abrasive bosses can become adequate bosses. Can abrasive bosses change their blind spots? Can they ever see that they harm others, and change their behavior? From my conversations with the people who manage them, I've learned that the leopard question reflects a deeply held belief that abrasive bosses are a hopeless lot. I've also learned that this belief is reinforced by management's well-meaning but failed attempts to intervene with abrasive bosses.

In the last chapter I described the top defense strategies managers use to avoid (flee) the threat of handling abrasive bosses. I've also had the opportunity over the years to talk with managers and human resource staff who steeled themselves to the challenge and did their best to intervene, with absolutely no success. The fact that they repeatedly tried and failed to bring about any change resulted in an unwavering conclusion that the situation was hopeless: "People don't really change." I encounter this belief every time I listen to the frustration of managers who have tried everything they can think of to get abrasive bosses to abandon their aggressive tactics. These desperate managers have tried disciplinary action, training, and referrals for counseling. Some have even resorted to flogging the offenders with abrasive yelling and name-calling. Nothing has worked, which has led them to conclude that abrasive bosses are hopeless:

"I've talked to him time and time again, but nothing changes."

"After I talked to her she improved for a while, but now we're back to square one."

"My words go in one ear and out the other. They just don't see—they just don't care."

When people ask me if abrasive bosses can change their behavior, I ask this question in response: "Have *you* ever changed *your* behavior?" Think about it—do you still behave exactly as you did in nursery school? In grade school? In high school? In your first job? Could it be true that you have never changed how you interact with others, in any way, in any context? I don't think so. If that were the case we'd all be taking diaper-change breaks at the office instead of coffee breaks. Think of all the times you've become (or been made) aware of one of your interpersonal blind spots and then corrected how you relate to others. This required change—from emotional blindness to emotional insight.

I am reminded of my very first job and my very first boss, Darryl Logan. A good man dedicated to doing good, he established the first employee assistance program (EAP) in Alaska. One day he decided to take this fledgling EAP counselor on a visit to a corporate client, during which I jokingly mentioned that "Darryl's desk is so disorganized—it's a miracle that he can ever find anything!" This style of sarcastic humor ran rampant in my family, and was executed by all family members with great skill and gusto. What boss wouldn't want to have a bright, witty employee like me on board?!

Not being the abrasive type, my boss was kind enough to enlighten me gently regarding my grossly inappropriate behavior. After the client meeting he calmly explained that portraying one's boss as less than competent to a customer did my company, my boss, and myself a disservice, something that this blind rookie had not realized until Darryl took my blinders off. I never did it again. I immediately saw that the caustic humor perceived as an expression of affection within my family was seen as disparaging and disrespectful in the business world. The blinders came off and *presto change-o!* One spot changed—only 185,426 to go.

You'll have a hard time convincing horse whisperers that out-of-control horses can't change, and you'll have an equally hard time trying to convince this boss whisperer that abrasive bosses can't temper their tempers. I base my belief that they *can* change not only on my experience as an executive coach and as an employee who stopped insulting her boss but also on my prior years of practicing psychotherapy and substance abuse intervention. I've seen people change. I've seen alcoholics stop drinking. I've seen parents stop abusing their children. I've seen people find ways to stop inflicting pain on themselves and others. This "can't change" logic doesn't work, because if people can't change, we must then conclude that all practitioners who engage in behavioral change are just bilking people of their money. I don't buy it—I've seen people change, and more specifically, I've seen and helped abrasive bosses change their blind spots and learn how to manage their employees without resorting to aggression.

See Spot Change

So how do people change their behavioral blind spots? There are numerous theories on how and why people change, but here's my conceptualization. To change their spots, people have to

1. *See* the blind spot (the abrasive behavior).
2. *Care* enough to change the behavior.
3. *Learn* how to change the behavior.

We've examined how bosses are blinder than bats: they either don't see their destructive behavior, or they see it but don't see the need to change it. Unable to see that their behavior is problematic, there is no motivation to change. So where does that leave you, the person who works over, under, or with an abrasive boss—sucked into the same black hole of darkness?

I struggled with this same question when I first encountered abrasive bosses blindly rubbing their coworkers the wrong way. How could I effect any change with these individuals? It was all too clear that if I wanted my clients to change and they were blind to the need to change, *nothing was going to change.* Therefore, to get my clients to change I had to take the following three steps:

1. Make them *see* the abrasive behavior.
2. Make them *care* enough to change the behavior.
3. Help them *learn* how to change the behavior.

Whoa, pardner—I can already see you bridling at my formula for handling abrasive bosses. I hear what you're saying: "You can't make people change if they don't want to! *You can lead a horse to water, but you can't make it drink.*" Technically, you are correct. You can't make people change or horses drink if they don't want to. But horse whisperers will be the first to tell you that you can present the horse with water (make it *see*) and work the horse until it's thirsty enough to want to drink (make it *care*). The same holds true for abrasive bosses: you can't make them change if they don't want to, but you can present them with feedback to make them see the wounds they inflict, and you can apply consequences that may make them care enough to want to change. The ultimate decision to drink from the well of change lies with the abrasive boss, but bosses (and horses) who choose not to drink run the risk of jeopardizing their survival.

The practice of making abrasive bosses see their behavior and care enough to change it doesn't involve rocket science.

Parents have been engaged in this practice with children ever since *Homo sapiens* opted for civilized behavior. For example:

1. The parent makes the child see the abrasive behavior: "Max, stop hitting your sister. You're hurting her!"
2. The parent makes the child care enough to change the behavior: "If you hit her again, you're going to your room."

Look familiar? It's the process of removing blinders and applying consequences. Max is made to see that his abrasive behavior is injurious to his sister and then, through the threat of exile, is made to care enough to want to stop it. Through this process one does one's best to make kids (or bosses or whomever) *see* their abrasive behavior, by pointing out the impact of the behavior, and then make them *care* enough to want to change the behavior, by applying consequences—by setting limits. Through embarrassing trials and many errors I discovered that these two steps are essential if there is to be any hope of change in abrasive bosses. But before I take you down that rocky road, I want to pause to address a question you may be asking, namely, who is responsible for step 3: helping abrasive bosses learn how to change the behavior? Here's the good news—*they* are.

If you want to see blind spots change, you will have to take the first two steps to make these bosses see and care enough to change their abrasive behavior. But step 3 is *their* responsibility—it's up to them to do whatever it takes to learn how to change their management style. Why isn't it your responsibility? Bottom line: your expertise is in the work you do, not in psychology. It's not your job to diagnose an individual's reliance on aggression in defense of his or her self-concept of supercompetence, nor is it your job to resolve the dysfunction. Consider the alcoholic employee whose work performance is deficient. It's not your job to diagnose or treat substance abuse. Your job is to make this employee see that his or her performance is deficient, and to make the employee care enough (by applying consequences for continued poor performance) to do what it takes to restore adequate performance. In this case it's the employee's responsibility to make the link between alcoholism and deteriorated work performance and to then seek help for substance abuse. It's up to the employee to *learn how* to stop drinking, ideally by seeking out people with expertise in that field. If the employee chooses not to get help and change, you at least have the peace of mind of knowing that you did your part—that you did what you could to bring about change.

In the same vein, it's not your job to diagnose and "fix" the underlying cause(s) of abrasive behavior. It *is* your job to try to make people *see* that their behavior is abrasive and to try to make them *care* enough by applying consequences for continued abrasion. After you've taken those steps, it's the abrasive boss's responsibility to learn how to manage interactions appropriately with coworkers. This is not to say that companies cannot be involved in supporting the learning process by funding coaching sessions or offering a health plan that covers psychotherapy. But remember the bottom line: you can lead a horse to see the water and you can make it want to drink, but *you can't make it drink.* The same holds for bosses. You can do your best to make them see and care enough to change, but *you can't make them change*—that's their choice.

Journey of a Greenhorn Boss Whisperer

I didn't set out originally to coach abrasive bosses. I started out coaching executives, managers, and supervisors on a variety of leadership development issues, such as decision making, team development, and other basic management skills. But what fascinated me were the interpersonal issues, the challenges of interacting with coworkers to make work truly work. I had some helpful advice to offer on the leadership development side, but I quickly discovered my true talent: helping bosses develop insight into why people behave as they do, and learn how to manage people to elicit desired behavior through positive means. That's why I founded the Executive Insight Development Group—to help leaders at all levels understand and manage the psychodynamics operating in their workplace. This focus generated more and more referrals of individuals who appeared to have little or no understanding of how emotions work at work, namely, abrasive bosses.

The referral would come as a brief telephone call from a manager or human resource specialist describing his or her concerns about an abrasive boss. The list of unacceptable behaviors could be very detailed, including specific consequences for failure to change: "He has a history of name-calling, of losing his temper and calling people names like 'idiot,' 'dimwit,' or 'clod.' We've talked to him about it, but he hasn't stopped. If he can't get control of this, we're going to have to proceed with disciplinary action and move toward termination." Armed with a picture of the boss's abrasive behaviors, I felt prepared to meet with the prospective client, convinced that we could get right down to business and work the miracle. Following introductions, I'd open with my first question:

> Coach: What is your understanding of why you were referred for coaching?
> Client: My boss thinks I'm too hard on people. He wants me to work on my communication skills.
> Coach: Too hard in what way?
> Client: He says that I push them too hard, but I don't agree. They need to be pushed or nothing would happen.
> Coach: What does "pushing too hard" mean?
> Client: I just tell them what they need to do—that's all.
> Coach: Did your supervisor give specifics on what he meant by "pushing too hard"?
> Client: Not really—he just said I had to be careful not to piss people off.

What was going on here? My client's supervisor had given me very specific information on the abrasive name-calling that led to the referral. Why was the client being so general? Didn't he see what he did? Why did he appear to have only a foggy vision of his manager's crystal-clear depiction of abrasion? And what was I going to do about it? As a greenhorn boss whisperer I naively stumbled forward into a major pitfall by specifying the abrasive boss's interpersonal crime—my feeble attempt to make him see his blind spots.

> Coach: Well, your boss told me that you call your cowork-
> ers names and that this has created a lot of distress.
> Client: That's not true—I don't know where he heard that.
> A lot of people have it in for me, and they're only saying
> this to bring me down. I did say once that only dimwits
> would think to ignore the product specs, but I wasn't
> directing that at anyone specific. Anyway, I don't see
> why he's making such a big deal of nothing.
> Coach: Oh ... uh ... uh ...
>   ... spluck
>   ... bluck
> [These are the giant sucking sounds of Coach sinking into a mud
> pit of ambiguity that she had initially believed to be solid ground of
> fact.]

Scraping the mud from my eyes, I saw that I had blindly stumbled into two coaching pitfalls:

1. *Management hadn't made them see.* Even when managers insist they've given abrasive bosses specific feedback on their unacceptable behavior(s), it usually hasn't been specific enough. And if managers do give detailed feedback, abrasive bosses will reject the feedback as invalid. They'll contest the facts.

2. *Management hadn't made them care.* Even though managers are convinced that they've set consequences for continued abrasive behavior, chances are good that they neglected to communicate those consequences.

From that day on I insisted on meeting with the referring party before entering the coaching corral with my client. I'd sit face to face with the abrasive boss's superiors and politely grill them on the specifics: "What exactly does the individual say or do that causes distress? What are the intended consequences if he or she doesn't stop? Exactly what has been said to the individual regarding consequences?" I'd spend a lot of time coaching managers on the importance of being specific when it came time to confront abrasive bosses, but it still wasn't enough—these managers *still* didn't make the abrasive bosses see. More often than not these emotionally blind individuals would continue to discount management's feedback, battling the facts of what did or didn't happen and denying the destructiveness of their disruptive behavior: "My manager wasn't there—he didn't see what happened. And he's making a mountain out of a molehill. Sometimes you have to get tough to get the job done—everyone knows that."

Straight from the Coworkers' Mouths

Thus far I had learned that management's input did little to make my clients see the disruptive effects of their behavior. Feedback helped but didn't totally remove their blinders because it wasn't perceived as *fact: "That's not what happened—you weren't there."* Faced with these emotionally blind (and now defensive) clients, I figured I'd have to gather even more feedback to try to penetrate their blindness. I wanted to interview the coworkers who were present when a client exhibited abrasive behavior—I wanted to hear it straight from their mouths. This was no easy task because the initial feedback I gathered from the abrasive boss's peers and subordinates was usually so general that I'd have to lead them into the specifics. For example:

Coach: I'm interested in your perceptions of how Rob interacts with coworkers.

Peer: Well, he can be a real pain to deal with. [*General description.*]

Coach: How so?

Peer: He gets defensive at the drop of a hat. [*Another general description.*]

Coach: Could you give me some examples?

Peer: Last week I asked Rob about a potential supplier. I'd been thinking of switching and wanted to get his input. He immediately got defensive. He said something like, "Don't you think I know what I'm doing?!" I wasn't questioning his judgment—I just wanted his help. It really pissed me off. [*Specific description.*]

Another example, this time from a subordinate:

Subordinate: Her communication skills stink. [*General description.*]

Coach: Could you give me more detail?

Subordinate: She interrupts a lot, particularly during brainstorming sessions. One person will be presenting their idea, and she'll break in with questions or what she thinks is a better idea. People just clam up—it's too much work to even get a word in. [*Specific description.*]

Each of these conversations started out with very general statements, but by asking for specific detail, I and my clients were able to see *exactly what they did or said that rubbed people the wrong way.* Both of the bosses in these examples were blindsided by their feedback. The first boss had no idea that he came across as defensive, and the second boss was shocked to see that what she viewed as impassioned participation was perceived as abrasive domination.

I'd like to say that these flashes of feedback resulted in miracle cures. They didn't—it took many more trips to the mud pit before I learned the fine points of boss whispering.

I offer my past challenges as a preview of coming distractions—of what you'll be up against if you attempt to tame the abrasive boss you work over, under, or with. Even when I was able to make my clients see their blind spots, it didn't necessarily make them care enough to want to change them. These people had spent years caring about management objectives—not about people's feelings. Their focus was on survival and, beyond survival, dominance in the dog-eat-dog world of business. Competence had ensured their survival, and supercompetence had gained them a degree of dominance in the organization's hierarchy. Why should they suddenly start caring about coworker *emotion* when years of caring about coworker *production* had ensured their business competence—their environmental fitness?

Climate Change

Consider the case of *Tyrannosaurus rex*, abrasive boss of Dinosauria, Inc. Former master of his domain, Rex failed to adapt to changes in his environment (the nature of which is still under debate), and the poor guy ended up one defunct dinosaur. The same case holds for abrasive bosses: their corporate climates are changing—there's a growing pressure to read and respect feelings. Companies are less willing to risk the costs of abrasive behavior and are increasingly insisting on the evolution of improved managerial styles. Those who fail to adapt to these new environmental pressures will suffer the same fate as ol' Rex—extinction.

My clients had already sensed this pressure change. They sensed that if they didn't soften up, they'd be shipped out. The magnitude of their maladaptation was revealed in their feedback reports—pages and pages describing employee distress and damaged work relationships. My clients could no longer deny the fact that despite their technical competence, their professional survival was jeopardized by these coworker and company perceptions of interpersonal *in*competence. Sensing this massive climate shift, these individuals were faced with the choice to abandon their primitive management styles for more adaptive approaches or face professional extinction. Could these bosses choose to change? *Can leopards change their spots?*

Where There's a Will, There's a Way: Evolution of Soft Spots

Leopards *can* change their spots—*they've been doing it for years*—millennia in fact. The twenty subspecies of *Panthera pardus* have evolved spots that put them at an advantage in their particular environments, from the huge spots of Thailand's clouded leopards to the nearly-black panthers of Southeast Asia, whose dark pelts provide excellent camouflage in shadowy tropical forests. This ability to adapt has given leopards *selective advantage*—those best adapted to their environments have a greater chance of surviving the forces of natural selection. Abrasive bosses, however, don't have thousands of years to evolve new behavioral patterns. Business environments change rapidly, and behaviors that were acceptable in another company or another era may prove maladaptive in one's current environment. We members of *Homo sapiens*, with our big brains and opposable thumbs, have proven to be highly adaptable creatures, capable of rapidly evolving new behaviors demanded by new companies, new management, and new legislation. However, the evolution of nonabrasive behaviors won't occur in abrasive bosses unless and until their business environments exert selective pressure, valuing technically *and* interpersonally competent management styles over technical competence alone.

If you manage an abrasive boss, you are in a position to exert this selective pressure by demanding the evolution of new spots—softer spots—namely, adequate management behaviors. You are the environmental force that can force the choice between survival and extinction. And if you work *under* an abrasive boss, there are ways to exert pressure both on your boss and on the surrounding management environment to bring about change. No matter whether you're the manager, subordinate, or peer of an abrasive boss, you'll have to take two steps to have any hope of seeing spots change—you'll have to do your best to make them *see* their blind spots and *care* enough to change them.

In the next three chapters I'll share what I've learned about making abrasive bosses see and care. I can tell you right now that taming an abrasive boss isn't easy, and as much as I'd like to, I can't guarantee your success. If you manage an abrasive boss, you may find that he or she is one of those who chooses not to change, and if you work for an abrasive boss, you may find that your company is one that chooses not to demand softer behaviors, despite your pleas. Subordinates and peers, please note: don't skip the next two chapters even though they are written for managers of abrasive bosses—you need to know what to expect of your company's management if you decide to exert pressure on *them*. Whether you work over, under, or with an abrasive boss, if you want to have the satisfaction of knowing that you did everything you possibly could to rein him or her in, the following chapters will show you what works, what doesn't, and why.

9

Blinders off

How Management Can Make Them See

Warning: lecture ahead. Sometimes in the course of a coaching session I'm suddenly struck with the urge to deliver a lecture. I'm fully aware of the fact that lecturing is outlawed as far as coaches are concerned—we're supposed to restrict ourselves to collaborative inquiry with our clients. This is my usual approach, but every so often I am overwhelmed with the impulse to speechify. I think my clients appreciate the fact that I secure their consent before dispensing my gems of insight, and I've forgiven the ones who rolled their eyeballs as I produced my portable soapbox from my briefcase. Because this is a book, I can't ask your permission, so please forgive me in advance for this two-minute lecture, titled

Turning a Blind Eye to Abrasion Is Unacceptable and Unethical

If you're a manager, you've got a responsibility beyond delivering your deliverables. It's your responsibility to manage both the performance and the *conduct* of your employees. Performance is *what* they do; conduct is *how* they do it—how they interact with others to fulfill their performance objectives. It's your responsibility to provide necessary resources and direction to your subordinates so that they can produce, *but it's also your duty as a manager to provide a respectful, nonabrasive work environment.* Turning a blind eye to workplace abrasion is unacceptable and unethical; it's your duty from a moral standpoint (as a leader of people) and from a business standpoint (as a leader of projects) to provide an interpersonally acceptable working environment. If you fail to do this, you will be perceived as weak and, worse, as tacitly condoning the abrasive behavior. You will be unable to build organizational bench strength for succession because valuable employees will jump ship. Escalating levels of distress will damage the productivity and viability of your organization as motivation drops and lawsuits loom. But worst of all, *you will be responsible for perpetuating workplace suffering,* suffering that harms the lives of your employees and their families.

Lecture over. Thanks—I feel better. Now let's get on with the first step of handling abrasive bosses from the manager's standpoint: taking their blinders off to make them see their damaging behavior.

Collecting Perceptions

If you want the abrasive boss to see the negative perceptions that he or she has generated, you'll have to start by making sure *you* see them. I've shared how I research the specifics of abrasive perceptions as part of my initial assessment. By the time I'm called in, the situation has deteriorated to the point where I have no difficulty locating the steaming piles of painful perceptions. In contrast, you, the abrasive boss's manager, may have gained awareness of the boss's abrasive behavior over a period of time, incident by disruptive incident. Because of this, you have the advantage of intervening at a much earlier point. Don't wait until you've amassed a perception pile of crisis proportions. Early intervention yields the highest return on investment, for two reasons. First, emotions aren't running as high in the early phases. You may encounter less defensiveness if the behaviors are addressed before much damage is done. Second, telling people promptly that they're generating unacceptable perceptions is not only your responsibility as a manager—*it's the polite thing to do.*

I learned this from my grandmother, who had an incredibly irritating habit of informing me of the social sins I committed— *long after the fact*: "Dolling [I'm descended from Brooklynites] ... I didn't want to tell you at the time, but when we were at the restaurant this evening you had a strip of toilet paper trailing from your shoe." *Thanks for not sharing, Grandma, !!*#%*. I can't help but hearken back to this early episode when my emotionally blind clients express their anger over not having been informed that they were trailing pained perceptions: "Why haven't I heard about this before? Apparently I've been pissing people off for a long time, but I've heard nothing until now. How was I supposed to know?!" Remember—*people can't change what they don't see*.

As soon as you get wind of an incident of abrasion, go see what *you* can see. This won't necessarily be easy. The abrasive boss's coworkers are going to have mixed feelings about sharing their perceptions. On the one hand they'll be impressed that you care enough to look into what happened. On the other hand they'll be fearful of retaliation from the boss if they speak openly with you. Here's my recommended approach for collecting perceptions in the face of this anxiety:

1. Explain that you've become aware of abrasion:
    "It's my understanding that there was some kind of incident in your department."
    "I'm aware that you're upset with your boss."
    "I heard something happened yesterday that stirred people up."
2. Explain that you want to get a clear picture of the incident(s):
    "I want to have a better understanding of what happened."
    "I need to know what occurred."
    "I'm trying to sort out what went on."

3. Explain your intent to help, not harm:

"I'm not interested in blaming—I'm interested in seeing what will help."

"I think it's important to understand what's going on."

"I'm not here to make the situation worse—I want to see what will make it better."

4. Seek specific detail on their perceptions:

"Tell me what happened, from your perspective."

"You said she got angry—specifically, what did she say or do?"

"What would I have seen or heard if I'd been there when it happened?"

5. Thank them for their input, and refrain from specific promises:

"Thanks for talking with me."

"This has been helpful—thanks."

"At this point I can't say what will happen, but I appreciate your input."

Beware the Hog-Tie Hitch

As you talk with people, avoid divulging anything you've already heard—coworkers and abrasive bosses both deserve the respect of an impartial and discreet exploration of the incident. Another important point: if coworkers express anxiety over getting into trouble with the boss for talking to you, assure them that retaliation is unacceptable and should be reported to you if it occurs. This brings us to a bind you may encounter when coworkers approach you regarding an abrasive incident, a bind I call the *hog-tie hitch*. An example:

"I need to tell you about something that happened with my boss last week, but I don't want him to know that

I came to talk to you. Here's what happened: when I
told him that I wasn't comfortable with his decision
to put me on another project, he glared at me and said
that if I 'didn't want to be treated like an incompetent
good-for-nothing, I should stop acting like one.' I didn't
say anything—I just left. I think you should know how
he talks to people—it's terrible."

Did you see it—the hog-tie hitch? *"But I don't want him
to know that I came to talk to you."* That's it—right there. The
employee wants you to do something about the incident, but the
hitch is that *you're not supposed to know about the incident.* If you
get roped into this, you've been hog-tied and should say so:

"I can understand that you don't want him to know that
you've brought this to me. But I need to let you know
about the bind this puts me in—I can't investigate the
incident, because you were the only person present and
Jack would immediately know it was you who brought
it forward. Under these circumstances, I can only file it
away and keep my eyes open for any further complaints.
That's not the direction I want to go. I'd prefer to look
into this now and make sure that people are treated with
respect. The company will not tolerate retaliation, but
the choice is yours. Which route do you want to take?"

Giving the employee the option of allowing you to look into
the incident is certainly not applicable where federal law requires
investigation, as in claims of sexual harassment or discrimination.
Under those circumstances you must investigate, whether or not
the complainant agrees. Consult with your HR specialist or legal
support. If investigation is not mandated, you'll want to do your
best to convince the coworker to let you intervene, and avoid
letting him or her hobble you with the hog-tie hitch.

All right—you've done it. You've collected coworker perceptions of abrasive behavior, and you're ready for the next step

of blinder removal: doing your best to make the abrasive boss see how he or she is perceived by presenting the perceptions you've compiled.

Presenting Perceptions

If you were lucky enough to get some management training in the course of your career, you'll remember the standard instructions for dealing with performance problems: "Once you have documented unacceptable performance, provide the employee with specific feedback"—usually followed by some advice about opening the conversation with a few positive comments and then proceeding to the negative feedback, including the admonition to *be specific.*

When you're dealing with performance problems, this is pretty good advice. Specific feedback shows the individual exactly what he or she is doing wrong. And it's not bad advice for addressing conduct problems as well. If you're going to take the blinders off to make abrasive bosses see exactly what elements of their conduct cause distress, vague won't work—fuzzy won't cut it. Foggy feedback only clouds vision—it won't help them see. I've learned that most of the feedback abrasive bosses get from their managers is too nebulous to be effective. These same managers will insist that they were very clear in communicating their concerns: "but it didn't help—*he still didn't get it.*" When I've asked them to recount precisely what they said to the abrasive boss, here's what they say:

> "I told him it would be a good idea to work on his communication skills."
>
> "I told her that she should rethink her management style."
>
> "I told him that he was alienating a lot of people and that he needed to do something about it."
>
> "I told her she needed to stop getting so defensive."

As I noted in the last chapter, I've repeatedly found that managers *think* they've been specific when they *haven't*. I could spend a few more paragraphs speculating on why this is, but I believe it boils down to two factors. First, there's the fear factor involved in taking bulls by the horns—the fear of being harmed or of doing harm. Second, I think that managers shy away from giving highly specific feedback about unacceptable conduct because it feels, well, *strange*. It's one thing to tell employees that they're not meeting deadlines—that's a very adult issue. It's another to tell them that they're misbehaving. Having to tell an abrasive boss to "behave" can be embarrassing; it's reminiscent of reprimanding a child who *didn't* learn all he or she really needed to know in kindergarten.

The task of presenting perceptions is further complicated by the fact that feedback, no matter how specific, won't necessarily guarantee that the abrasive boss will see the need to change. You can whisper yourself blue in the face telling an abrasive boss the exact specifics of what he said or did that caused distress, and chances are you won't get anywhere. Contrary to popular belief, specifics alone are unlikely to take the blinders off and make them see. To clarify, let me first present you with this fantasy version of giving specific feedback:

> *Manager:* John, I wanted to meet with you today to discuss complaints I've received regarding your conduct with coworkers. I heard that in a meeting with your team last week, you shouted at them and threatened to fire them. One person said that you told them that if they couldn't do the job, you'd find people who could. I've had a steady stream of people in my office since then.
>
> *Abrasive Boss:* I never said that. That's not what happened.
>
> *Manager:* That's what was reported to me.
>
> *Abrasive Boss:* Oh. Forgive me—if that's what you were told, then it must be fact. It was wrong of me, and I won't do it again. Thanks for sharing—I appreciate it.

Hey—that was easy! The manager just stood his ground, and the abrasive boss saw the light. And if you believe this scenario represents reality, you're working at Fantasyland, Inc. I hate to break it to you, but if you think you can make abrasive bosses see what they do simply by giving them specific feedback and standing your ground, you're going to get a *KITH* (a kick in the head) as you try to take their blinders off. This is neither a pleasant nor a productive experience, so let me explain how to avoid being blindsided.

Don't Forget You're a Threat

Let's look first at the process of taking the blinders off a horse. If the horse perceives you as a threat, it will resist. It will back off (flee) or kick (fight). The same holds for abrasive bosses—if they perceive you as a threat, they will resist. So how is it that you, a concerned manager willing to take on the challenge of taming an abrasive boss, could be perceived as a threat? To put it bluntly, *you are going to be telling people who perceive themselves as competent that they are in fact incompetent*—interpersonally incompetent. And the moment you try to remove their blinders and make them see that they are interpersonally incompetent, *you, their manager, become a threat to their sense of competence, and threats must be defended against.* Remember the survival dynamic: threat → fear → defense? The threat of being perceived as incompetent will generate intense anxiety in the abrasive boss, and this anxiety will activate vigorous defense against the threat—in other words, against *you.* You may think you are standing on solid ground, well equipped with your very specific feedback, but watch what happens in the real world:

> *Manager:* John, I wanted to meet with you today to discuss complaints I've received regarding your conduct with coworkers. I heard that in a meeting with your team last week, you shouted at them and threatened to fire

them. One person said that you told them that if they couldn't do the job, you'd find people who could. I've had a steady stream of people in my office since then.

Abrasive Boss: I never said that. That's not what happened.

Manager: That's what was reported to me.

Abrasive Boss: Well, that's not what happened. I didn't shout at them—I just made it clear that our customers won't tolerate second-rate work, and that things have to change.

Manager: Oh . . . uh . . . uh . . .

　　　　　　. . . spluck

　　　　　　　　　. . . bluck

[*Giant sucking sounds of Manager sinking into mud pit of ambiguity that he had initially believed to be solid ground of fact.*]

Manager (inhaling deeply): The fact is that people said they were threatened.

Abrasive Boss: That's just their perception. I'm telling you the facts—what really happened.

Manager: Well . . .

　　　　　　. . . spluck

　　　　　　　　　. . . bluck

[*Total silence.*]

(*Final score: Abrasive Boss, 1; Manager, 0.*)

So much for standing on the solid ground of fact. Manager has done a good job of presenting the specific behaviors that are *perceived* as abrasive, but Abrasive Boss defends against the threat of being seen as abrasive (and thus incompetent) by *battling* the facts. Battling the facts of a situation is a remarkably effective defense, especially in the business world where facts carry tremendous weight. In business, facts are consistently valued over feelings: we are expected to base our business decisions on solid fact, not on squishy feelings. Because of this, *battling the facts of what happened in an abrasive episode is a very effective defensive maneuver.* Manager's valiant efforts to make

Abrasive Boss see the impact of his behavior got mired in the mud, and Abrasive Boss will blindly labor on, the next emotional collision only a matter of time.

Hearing Hearsay

Let's climb out of the mud pit and take another look at this phase of taming abrasive bosses. I've talked about the fact that vague hints won't penetrate their emotional blindness. I've also presented the fact that specific feedback on the abrasive boss's behavior will be met with defensiveness—you'll get bogged down in fact battles of what really happened, who said what, who did what, and so on. And here's another fact: in most cases, *you weren't there*. You weren't there to see exactly what was said or done, so the fact is that *you are standing on shaky ground when you try to make abrasive bosses see that their behavior wounds*. Managers often see this last fact as justification for not intervening with abrasive bosses:

> "I can't confront him on this because it's all based on hearsay."
>
> "When it comes down to it, it's the employee's word against hers. That's not enough to go on."
>
> "Who can say what really happened? I wasn't there, so I don't know."

Sorry, but I don't buy this justification. If you're waiting until you have an opportunity to observe an abrasive boss's injurious behavior directly, you may be waiting a long, long time. Many of my clients were perfectly appropriate in their behavior with their superiors and abrasive only with their subordinates and/or peers. So here's my question for you: how many reports of abrasive behavior do you plan to ignore until you decide to take *your* blinders off? In many cases it's not until the company is hit with a hostile environment action that employee *hearsay* is suddenly legitimized as an employee *report* of harassment. I don't get it—federal law requires managers to treat reports of discrimination or sexual harassment very seriously. How, then, can managers profess support for investigating these forms of abrasion while dismissing reports of other manifestations of abrasion as hearsay? Uh-oh . . . I feel another lecture coming on. But I'll spare you and return instead to the challenge of taking an abrasive boss's blinders off. How do you, as a manager, go about making individuals see their abrasive behavior and the friction that results?

What Works: Presenting Feeling as Fact

Our mud-covered Manager did a fine job of focusing Abrasive Boss on the specific behaviors that were perceived as abrasive by coworkers. But that wasn't enough, because Abrasive Boss challenged him on the facts of what happened. To take the blinders off, Manager will have to win this battle by redefining "fact." In this strategy, facts do not refer to *events*—facts refer to *feelings*. Follow these two simple steps:

1. Focus on *feelings*, not facts.
2. And then present feelings as *facts*.

In this approach, you first focus the abrasive boss on the specific behaviors that coworkers *perceive* as abrasive. Then, faster than a speeding bullet, you assert the *fact* that these coworkers *feel* they are being treated disrespectfully. Here's how it works:

> *Manager:* John, I wanted to meet with you today to discuss complaints I've received regarding your conduct with coworkers. I heard that in a meeting with your team last week, you shouted at them and threatened to fire them. One person said that you told them that if they couldn't do the job, you'd find people who could. I've had a steady stream of people in my office since then.

[*Step 1 completed—specific description of perceived abrasive behaviors.*]

Abrasive Boss: I never said that. That's not what happened. [*Defense against threat of being perceived as incompetent.*]

Manager: That's what was reported to me.

Abrasive Boss: Well, that's not what happened—you weren't there. I didn't shout at them—I just made it clear that our customers won't tolerate second-rate work and that things have to change. [*Defensive launch of fact battle.*]

Manager: John, the fact is that I don't know and cannot know exactly what happened—I wasn't there. But I do know one fact: your people felt that they were treated disrespectfully. [*Step 2 completed—feeling presented as fact.*]

There it is—*feeling* presented as *fact*. In this example, Manager has avoided the pitfall of debating the facts of what happened by shifting the battle to the irrefutable *facts* of how employees *feel* about Abrasive Boss's abrasive behavior. If you want to take an abrasive boss's blinders off, vague feedback won't work, nor will specific feedback unless it attests to the facts of coworker feelings, facts that you, the manager, are now focusing the abrasive boss on—facts that you are making him or her see. This is the exact strategy I use to make my abrasive clients see the negative perceptions generated by their abrasive behavior—hovering like horseflies and sucking the lifeblood out of their credibility as competent bosses.

In my role of executive coach, I can't and won't get bogged down in debating what happened, who said what, who is to blame, and the like. Just like you—*I wasn't there.* I'll never know exactly what happened, but I do know for a *fact* that my client is surrounded by the pained perceptions of the working wounded. The bottom line is that an abrasive boss's description of the facts or circumstances of the abrasive moment is irrelevant; the fine distinctions of whether Abrasive Boss shouted at his people or just "made it clear" are immaterial. *What counts is the undeniable, unavoidable, incontestable fact that coworkers feel wounded by the abrasive boss*, a boss who leaves a trail of tears, a beaten path of bruises, a wake of wounds. Take it from this boss whisperer's experience, gained from years of making abrasive bosses see: they may defend against the fact that they *are* abrasive, but they have no defense against the more important fact that they are *perceived* to be abrasive.

I remember sitting with a client who was grappling with the distressed perceptions contained in his feedback summary. He, as many clients do, was still focused on *his* perception of the facts of what happened in his interactions with coworkers: "I never said that—I never meant to insult them. I was just trying to get them to wake up and see the realities of what we're up against." As I listened, I was suddenly struck with an image of five enormous horseflies hovering over his head, each roughly the size of a grapefruit. They buzzed about slowly, prepared to bite him at any moment. I shared this image with my client—an imaginative sort:

"Peter, these flies are the negative perceptions that trail you wherever you go these days. You don't know where they come from, you don't know what caused most of them, and you obviously don't know how to get rid of them. They keep buzzing around—the old ones don't die off, and they seem to be multiplying. And on top of it all, these negative perceptions do you damage. They're like horseflies—they bite, and when they bite, they take a chunk out of you. They're sucking the lifeblood from your career—they're damaging your reputation, your credibility, and perhaps even your ability to survive at this company. And no matter how hard you try to get rid of them, they just keep coming back to bite. You don't understand where these negative perceptions come from or how to get rid of them—permanently—so that they don't come back to bite you. That's where I come in: I see it as my job to help you understand and eliminate these perceptions, to manage them out of existence. I'm here to make you more effective than you already are, without paying the price you're paying right now."

Pretty good sales pitch for change, if I do say so myself. (That's the advantage of writing a book—you can "say so yourself" as much as you want.) The pitch works every time, because I hold out the promise of making the boss *more* effective, *more* powerful—a promise that appeals to his or her drive for supercompetence. It also works because I've shifted the whole focus from, "You need coaching because you make people suffer," to, "You need coaching because *you're* suffering from these negative perceptions." Here's the bottom line: I have no interest in debating the facts of whether an abrasive boss does harm. I'm only interested in the fact that the abrasive boss is *perceived* as doing harm, perceptions that are now buzzing back to bite.

Disarming Defenses

You, the manager, are ready to confront the abrasive boss. You've memorized steps 1 and 2 of presenting feeling as fact and you're rarin' (well, maybe not exactly *rarin'*, but you're ready) to take the blinders off. You've consulted with your human resource specialist, you've scheduled a private meeting with the abrasive boss (because you don't believe in the practice of public humiliation), you've calmed yourself (also a requirement for horse and boss whisperers), and you're ready to make the abrasive boss see

- The specific behaviors that are *perceived* as abrasive by coworkers
- The *fact* that coworkers *feel* they are being treated disrespectfully

Hold your horses for a moment—don't forget that you're about to become a threat. You're about to threaten the abrasive boss's self-image of competence, a threat that may be fiercely defended against. I want to prepare you to overcome this defensiveness, and I also want you to understand that abrasive bosses will resist your efforts to make them see and make them care, not because they are evil, but because they are *afraid*. As we've discussed, abrasive bosses are unconsciously fearful of being perceived as incompetent, because of past anxiety-provoking experiences in their home, school, or work lives. Somehow, somewhere, they learned that being seen as competent was all-important, and the possibility of being perceived as incompetent threatens the survival of their self-esteem. For the majority of abrasive bosses I've coached, the specter of incompetence constitutes not only a conscious threat to their professional dominance but an unconscious threat to their psychological survival as well.

Your objective in taking the blinders off is to make abrasive bosses see that *they are perceived as a threat to coworkers*. As you focus abrasive bosses on these negative perceptions, *you in turn will be seen as a threat* to their self-image of competence. Your words will arouse intense anxiety and a variety of defensive responses, all designed to ward off the deeply distressing unconscious threat of incompetence, representing weakness and failure. You'll need to disarm these defenses as you work to penetrate their emotional blindness and shed light on the injury they inflict on coworkers, their company, and themselves.

As you enter this not-so-OK corral, you'll be sorely tempted to fight fire with fire. Be advised—in most cases, abrasive bosses will fight back against the threat of being portrayed as interpersonally incompetent. They will marshal an artillery of defenses to detonate your perceptions. And when you feel attacked, there's a natural tendency to attack back. If you're going to get through their line of defense, *you will have to restrain your understandable impulses to react aggressively*. Remember that you are doing these bosses a favor—you're alerting them to the damage they are doing to others and, ultimately, themselves. You're helping them see their blind spots in the hope that they will develop insight. This, of all times, is the time to exercise empathy—to put yourself in their shoes and understand their fear of being seen as incompetent, inadequate, a failure. In other words, when taking the blinders off wild horses or abrasive bosses, approach with care, and care enough to do your very best.

The three most common defenses deployed by abrasive bosses against the threat of being perceived as incompetent are *denial*, *projection*, and *rationalization*. Here's a brief summary of how these defenses work and what you'll hear.

- *Denial.* The abrasive behavior will be dismissed as untrue, as nonfactual:

  "That's not what I said."

  "That's not what I did."

  "That's not what happened."

- *Projection.* The abrasive behavior will be blamed on others:

  "They pushed my buttons." (*It's their fault.*)

  "You don't give me the resources I need to get the job done." (*It's your fault.*)

  "These deadlines are unrealistic." (*It's the company's fault.*)

- *Rationalization.* The abrasive behavior will be justified as reasonable:

  "I had to do it to get people moving." (*It's necessary.*)

  "We can't afford to screw up this project." (*It's noble.*)

  "I'm not the only one around here who does it." (*It's common.*)

As you encounter these defensive statements in the course of taking abrasive bosses' blinders off, keep in mind that *they believe what they're saying*—they're not trying to pull the blinders over your eyes. They honestly believe that they weren't being abrasive or that they were forced to be abrasive in the best interests of the company. So don't make the mistake of getting defensive when you hear these defensive responses—if you do, all is lost. Just remember the key steps to making abrasive bosses see what they do. Focus them on

- The specific behaviors that are *perceived* as abrasive by coworkers
- The *fact* that their coworkers *feel* they are being treated disrespectfully

Remember, the goal is *not* to make abrasive bosses agree that they are abrasive. You won't succeed. They'll battle the facts of what they did or said and insist that they weren't interpersonally incompetent. Instead, the goal is to make them see that they are *perceived* as abrasive. The distinction is crucial. Trying to make them see that they are abrasive will mire you in the mud pit of defensive debate, but making them see the distressed perceptions they generate puts you on very solid ground. Here are some examples of how this subtle shift in focus effectively disarms the defenses of denial, projection, and rationalization that you're almost sure to encounter.

Disarming Denial

If you deny something, it doesn't exist. You don't have to deal with it, because there's no *it* to deal with. Denial doesn't necessarily imply deception—sometimes the ol' unconscious kicks in to protect us from information too threatening to deal with on a conscious level. That's what makes denial such a great defense. You can make the problem go away by denying there's any problem at all.

The "I Didn't Say It" Denial

Manager: John, I wanted to meet with you today to discuss complaints I've received regarding your conduct with coworkers. I heard that in a meeting with your team last week, you shouted at them and threatened to fire them. One person said that you told them that if they couldn't do the job, you'd find people who could. I've had a steady stream of people in my office since then.

Abrasive Boss: That's not what I said—I just made it clear that our customers won't tolerate second-rate work and that things have to change.

Manager: That may not be exactly what you said—I wasn't there. But the fact is that you were *perceived* as saying it—people took whatever you said as a direct threat to their jobs.

The "I Didn't Do It" Denial

Abrasive Boss: I didn't do that—I didn't tell them that I was going to fire them. I just wanted to light a fire under them.

Manager: You may feel you didn't threaten their jobs, but *they* felt you did. And let me tell you, I don't believe in management by incineration—people end up feeling burned, and that's not how I want our employees to feel.

The "That's Not What Happened" Denial

Abrasive Boss: That's not what happened—they're blowing it all out of proportion. They're making a big deal out of nothing.

Manager: Something happened, or I wouldn't be getting these complaints. And whatever happened—whatever you said or did—it's creating a lot of distress. I've gotten similar complaints in the past—people feeling intimidated and alienated because of the way you treat them.

Disarming Projection

Projection is a common workplace strategy for defending against unconsciously threatening input. One simply deflects the incoming mental missile back to its sender: "It's not *my* issue—it's *your* issue."

The "It's Their Fault" Projection

Abrasive Boss: They pushed my buttons—that's why I lost it.

Manager: That's no justification for launching a nuclear attack. As a manager, you're expected to deal with difficult employees without attacking them. It's called *managing*, not mangling.

The "It's Your Fault" Projection

Abrasive Boss: You don't give me the resources I need to get the job done.

Manager: I won't accept that as a reason for treating people badly. If you're feeling up against the wall, I expect you to bring that to me. I'm here to work with you to figure out how to do more with less—we're all up against that wall—but it doesn't justify calling in the firing squad.

The "It's the Company's Fault" Projection

Abrasive Boss: These deadlines are unrealistic.

Manager: I agree that we're getting hit with some very tough timelines, but that's no excuse for treating people disrespectfully. No matter how hard the going gets, you're going to get more out of people if you treat them with respect, and that's my expectation.

Disarming Rationalization

With rationalization, the powers of reason are deployed to justify one's actions. Seemingly reasonable reasoning can take a number of forms: favored defensive dodges include the ends-justify-the-(mean)-means and the all-the-other-kids-do-it gambits.

The "It's Necessary" Rationalization

Abrasive Boss: I had to do it to get people moving.

Manager: If kicking people is the only way you can get people to move, you're going to have to find another way. I'm here to help you with that. The next time you want to drop-kick an employee through the goalposts of work, talk to me first.

The "It's Noble" Rationalization

Abrasive Boss: We can't afford to screw up this project.

Manager: You're absolutely right. And we can't afford to have angry, demoralized employees who are thinking of quitting instead of pulling off this project.

The "It's Common" Rationalization

Abrasive Boss: I'm not the only one around here who does it.

Manager: I don't disagree, but we're here today to talk about you, not them. And to be frank, I know I'm not perfect in this department, but I've worked hard to change. You're the only person who can control how you treat others, and I'm expecting you to do that.

Disarming Miscellaneous Defensive Dodges

Here are some additional defensive strategies you may encounter in your efforts to take the blinders off:

Abrasive Boss: You don't understand what I'm up against.

Manager: I may not understand what you're up against, but I do understand that you're not handling it acceptably. If you have problems you can't solve, you need to be talking with me.

Abrasive Boss: You've never said anything about this before.

Manager: I didn't really see that it was a problem before. When it first happened, I though it was a one-time incident. But I'm starting to see a pattern here, and it's not OK.

Abrasive Boss: You're making a big deal out of nothing—it's not that bad.

Manager: You may see it as nothing, and you're right: I do see it as a big deal. And you're going to have to decide whose perception is more important—yours or mine. That's your decision.

Abrasive Boss: I didn't do anything to her—she's just got it in for me.

Manager: This isn't the first complaint ever made about you. Your behavior has been an issue with other people in the past. You say that a lot—"they've got it in for me." Has it ever occurred to you that people have it in for you because you've come after them?

Abrasive Boss: You're just trying to get rid of me.

Manager: I don't want to get rid of you. I want you here because of your [*list positive qualities*]. But I won't tolerate this unacceptable behavior. Your behavior is in your hands, not mine—it's up to you.

Abrasive Boss: So since when did this become a crime?

Manager: Since now. We cannot and will not tolerate this behavior.

Abrasive Boss: But I did this all the time at my past company [or before you were my boss] and no one ever said anything.

Manager: That was then. This is now.

Abrasive Boss: I run the top-performing department. I've done more for this company than anyone else around here.

Manager: That's true. In terms of performance, you're at the top. But that's not enough—we expect acceptable conduct as well as acceptable performance. You get great results, but the ends don't justify the means. We don't want to get hit with harassment complaints, and I don't want to see our employees suffer at your hands.

Abrasive Boss: How do you expect me to get anywhere with a bunch of incompetents?

Manager: If you have employees who are not capable of doing the job, I expect you to deal with that without yelling at them. You hired them or inherited them and decided to keep them on, and it's your job to manage them without creating all this emotional distress. If they're incompetent, I expect you to find out why and deal with it instead of yelling at them. Do they need training, resources, discipline, direction? What's your role in this?

Abrasive Boss: I'm not going to sit around and listen to this—I've got work to do.

Manager: You don't have to listen to this—that's your choice. But "this" isn't going to go away, and I'm not going to pretend it doesn't exist. I want to know if and when you'll be ready to listen.

Abrasive Boss: This is crap—and you're full of crap.

Manager: That may be how you see it, but I'm not willing to continue this discussion if you're going to use that kind of language. I'll see you here first thing tomorrow, and I expect you to be civil.

Please remember that having one's blinders removed can be very painful—put yourself into your abrasive boss's shoes and think back to times when you were made to see the negative perceptions you'd created—the behavioral toilet paper stuck to *your* shoes. Once you've taken the blinders off and made abrasive bosses see what they do, it's time to make them care—by setting limits with care.

10

Limits on

How Management Can Make Them Care

In the last chapter I described the steps managers must take to take the blinders off:

- Collect the perceptions of abrasion.
- Present the wounded feelings as facts.
- Disarm defensiveness.

You've collected and reflected the wounded perceptions that are now disrupting work—you've done your best to pry off the abrasive boss's emotional blinders with the irrefutable *fact* that he or she is perceived as abrasive. These individuals may attempt to continue to debate the facts of whether or not they behaved abrasively, but because you've shifted the focus from a fact battle over what they did (or didn't) do, to the *facts of how they are perceived*, you've increased your chances of disarming their defenses. You've done your best to make them see: congratulations on your hard work.

Next: Limits on

You're not done yet. The time has come to do your best to make the abrasive boss care enough to want to change. To give it your best shot, you'll now have to

- Make the business case for caring.
- Threaten consequences for continued abrasion.
- Offer help.

From the beginning of my boss whispering days, the first step of taming abrasive bosses (taking the blinders off) came pretty easily—all I had to do was interview the abrasive boss's coworkers to capture an overwhelming swarm of painful perceptions generated by his or her behavior. I vividly recall the day that I arrived in a high-level executive's office to present the plethora of pained perceptions gnawing away at his effectiveness and credibility. I warned him—as I do all of my clients—that he might find his feedback disturbing, but he brushed me (and the perceptions) off with: "Don't be silly. There's nothing they could say that would bother me. Let's get on with it." The "silly" accusation didn't exactly rub my feelings the right way, but stifling an impulse to retort, "This is going to hurt *you* a lot more than it's going to hurt *me*," I instead produced his lengthy (twelve single-spaced pages in font size 10) feedback summary, which depicted in graphic detail the deep frustration, anger, and despair experienced by his coworkers in response to his aggression. Seeing for the first time the magnitude of the pain he'd inflicted, he literally clutched at his chest and choked out, "Oh my God—*you were right*. This is the worst day of my professional life." So much for "silly"—as soon as the blinders came off and his eyes were opened, he cared. He cared enough to want to change and worked hard from that point on to improve his management style.

I found this immediate reparative reaction to be the exception rather than the rule. For most of my clients, seeing that their behavior was emotionally disruptive was *not* enough to make them want to change. As I noted earlier, they had spent years caring about work objectives and not workplace emotions, attaining dominance through their dogged pursuit of top-dog status. How could I rein in these hard-charging, hard-hitting, hard-nosed bosses? Just taking the blinders off usually didn't cut it—making them want to change would require an ironclad case for interpersonal competence.

Making the Business Case

This step wasn't going to be easy. It didn't take me long to figure out that the it's-not-nice-to-hurt-others argument wouldn't work with this crowd. They had been raised in environments where feelings were ignored or devalued, resulting in their emotional blindness. How could I make a hard case for these soft skills without revealing my mission to reduce workplace suffering? That approach would only get me booted out the door reserved for time-wasting, touchy-feely types. Baffled, my bleeding-heart social worker side consulted my cold-hearted executive side, which icily informed me that if I wanted to make my clients change, I would have to make a solid *business case for caring*. And therein lay the challenge: how do you sell the concept of caring for others' feelings to those who have no interest in your product?

I'll cut to the chase and tell you how I did this. First, I constructed my case in proper (emotion-free) business language, avoiding words like *nice*, *caring*, and *kind* at all costs. Second, I avoided any temptation to lecture and instead immediately shifted into Socratic whispering, asking these abrasive bosses to conduct a cost-benefit analysis of their abrasive behavior:

"What are the benefits of your current management style— of [*list of specific abrasive behaviors*]?"
   "It wakes people up and shows that I'm serious."
   "It makes them see that they're not doing what they're supposed to do."
   "It motivates them to step it up."
   "It shows them who's in charge."

"It makes them stop doing whatever they shouldn't be doing."

"It gets the job done faster and more efficiently."

"And as of today, what price have you paid for your aggressive management style?"

"People don't want to work for me."

"They've gotten me in trouble with HR."

"I've been told I won't get a promotion."

"Someone's brought legal action against the company."

"I could lose my job."

"I have to waste time meeting with you."

I loved the last comment—there's nothing like an endearing insult from a prospective client to get my bleeding-heart blood boiling with these unspoken words: *Just you wait—by the time I get done with you, you'll be empathizing with the best of them, and you'll enjoy every minute of it!*"

To make abrasive bosses care enough to want to change, you need to put them through the paces of calculating the costs of *not* caring about others' emotions. They understand and accept this businesslike approach, and as they compare the costs and benefits of their management styles, it becomes clear that the short-term benefits of abrasive behavior that *they* see (attainment of business goals) are far outweighed by the long-term costs that you are *making them see* (damage to employee and organizational functioning). In the course of conducting this analysis, the abrasive boss will also see that this negative trend is extremely dangerous in terms of survival: the aggression that intimidated workers into action is now threatening the abrasive boss's dominance and survival in the work environment.

Making the business case for interpersonal competence is an essential step in handling abrasive bosses. Calmly weighing the benefits of technical competence against the costs of interpersonal incompetence will set the stage for the next step: demanding change. You're about to make it clear that the days of threatening and intimidating coworkers are over: the time has come to make them care enough to choose to change.

Threatening Consequences for Continued Abrasion

To get horses headed in the right direction, horse whisperers not only take the blinders off—they also put a bridle on. Bridles are effective equine management tools because they incorporate a threat mechanism, namely, the bit. If Thunderbolt bolts off in the wrong direction, the whisperer simply reins him in, exerting pressure on the bit in the horse's mouth—an aversive experience. Very soon the slightest tug on the reins will bring Thunderbolt into line, because he now has the horse sense to avoid repeating his past experience of gum grief. There's that ol' survival dynamic in action again: threat $\rightarrow$ fear $\rightarrow$ defense, here manifested as pressure on reins $\rightarrow$ fear of pain $\rightarrow$ defensive flight into compliance.

To make bosses see, you show them the destructive perceptions generated by their abrasive behavior. Then, to make them care, you show them the destructive consequences of any future abrasive behavior. To put it bluntly, *you have to threaten them*. You have to threaten their professional survival to stimulate anxiety sufficient to make abrasive bosses want to change; you're going to threaten them with the consequences of continuing their unacceptable behavior. At first glance, threatening people would seem to be a rather uncivilized recommendation, but if we hearken back to the survival dynamic of both natural and corporate jungles, you will recall that threats to survival are defended against through either flight or fight. *The goal here is to threaten abrasive bosses' organizational survival and escalate their anxiety to the point where they feel compelled to flee (abandon) their abrasive style* in favor of a more humane approach: pressure on profession

→ fear of firing (or some variation on that theme) → defensive flight into compliance.

Threatening people could imply that you too must behave abrasively—not so. Threats can be presented gently—yanking on the reins and yelling are not required. Physicians do it all the time, quietly presenting the threat of lung cancer to smokers and calmly informing their diabetic patients of the threat from sugar consumption. Parents thoughtfully present real-world threats to their children: "You have to look both ways before crossing the street—you could be hit by a car." There's no need to thrash an abrasive boss with the threat imposed by his or her abrasive behavior. You can make the individual see the future consequences of not caring about coworker emotions by calmly threatening his or her continued survival in your workplace. Here's the basic threat template:

> "We cannot and will not tolerate this behavior—if it doesn't stop, I will be forced to take action."

That's it—no yelling, no yanking, no flogging—just the quiet fact that you're setting limits on the abrasive boss's behavior. You exert pressure to threaten abrasive bosses into abandoning their aggressive management style and to respectfully intimidate them into pursuing interpersonal competence. I prefer this template because it implies that both you (the abrasive boss's manager) and the organization ("we") are setting the limit. Here are some variations on the theme, all voiced in a calm, concerned tone:

> "We cannot condone your treatment of employees. Your management approach is unacceptable and will have to change—now."

> "We will not risk being sued for the hostile environment you're creating—this cannot go on."

> "This continual stream of negative perceptions has to end. If you can't turn things around, I'll have to do what it takes to make it happen."

"We want employees to *want* to come to work, and yours don't—this cannot continue."

"Our code of conduct calls for respect of others. If you can't bring your behavior into compliance with that code, I'll be forced to take action."

There—you've done it: you've taken the blinders off and put the limits on. And you've done it with empathy, putting yourself into the abrasive boss's anxious and understandably defensive shoes as you quietly convey the threatening consequences of continued abrasion. There's no need to shout—that's why they call it boss *whispering*.

For Every Action There Will Be a Reaction

You've now threatened to take action against abrasive behavior. A cautionary note: *do not make empty threats*. Don't even think of reining in an abrasive boss if you're not willing to have him or her suffer the consequences of behaving abrasively toward others. The goal here is to shift the suffering from your employees to the abrasive boss: to make the aggressors see that they—not their employees—will suffer the wounds of any further attacks. Empty threats can have disastrous consequences for you, because in failing to follow through with the consequences you've threatened, you will be perceived as weak, incompetent, and thus irrelevant by the abrasive boss. There's no faster way to demote yourself in the dominance hierarchy—don't say this boss whisperer didn't warn you.

Speaking of the great minds of Western civilization, Sir Isaac Newton stated in his third law of motion that *for every action there is an equal, but opposite, reaction*. This law also applies to handling abrasive bosses: for every abrasive action by the boss, there must be an equal, but nonabrasive, reaction by the organization. This rules out the eye-for-an-eye concept of retributive justice, an approach that Mahatma Gandhi observed "makes the whole world blind." Retribution doesn't apply here; instead, further abrasive *actions* should be met with civilized disciplinary *reactions*. In the early phases of intervention it's not necessary to specifically define your next reaction to abrasive action—I've seen many abrasive bosses shape up immediately in response to the ambiguous threat implied in the "I will be forced to take action" statement. That's all they needed to drink from the well of change—no further elaboration was necessary. If your abrasive boss demands further detail, don't feel compelled to comply. You don't want to lock yourself into a specific reaction before you've researched the abrasive action and consulted with your human resource specialist. Instead, you can make general reference to the fact that your company has a disciplinary process (I hope) that will be followed. Ambiguity (generating fear of the unknown) can sometimes produce more motivation to change than threats of specific consequences.

We're Doing This for Your Own Good

By taking the blinders off and putting the limits on, you'll trigger your abrasive boss's deepest fear—*the threat of being perceived as incompetent*. True to the survival dynamic, he or she will defend against the perception of interpersonal incompetence through fight or flight. In the fight scenario, abrasive bosses will attempt to fight against the negative perceptions of coworkers or your demand for change, or both. In the last chapter we discussed how to disarm defenses against negative perceptions, but if these disarmament strategies fail and your abrasive boss refuses to change—*chooses* not to change—treat that choice with respect. Don't bother to fight back, because there's no point in taking bull-headed bosses by the horns a second time—they've marked themselves for exile or extinction. We'll explore this scenario in greater detail in Chapter Twelve.

Once you've put the limits on, don't be surprised if the abrasive boss responds to your threat with his or her own threat to flee the scene: "I don't need to put up with this—I'm out of here." This is a critical moment. It's your opportunity to make clear that you don't want to exterminate the abrasive boss—you just want him or her to exterminate the abrasive behavior. Don't let the individual leave your office or your company without stating this very explicitly:

> "It is not my intent to have you leave, Carol. If I wanted
> to get rid of you, I could have done that long ago.
> I *don't*—you bring tremendous value to this com-
> pany, and I really appreciate all of the time and energy
> you've invested in our success. I want you here for the
> long haul, but only if you can treat your coworkers
> with respect. And I'm realistic—I don't expect you
> to know exactly how to straighten this out overnight.
> We want to offer you help to do that."

Setting limits with an abrasive boss will be less threatening to you if you understand that you're not doing it just to protect your company—you're also working in the boss's best interests. You're presenting the threat of organizational extinction to help rather than harm. You *want* this person to survive in your company, or you would have found a way to fire the individual a long time ago. You *want* this person's technical expertise, which enhances your company's fitness. You *want* the situation to work, and to do that, your abrasive boss will have to choose to make it work. Here's how I phrase it from my boss whisperer's perspective:

> *Abrasive Boss:* I can't believe they're threatening to get rid
> of me if I don't change my management style. I've done
> everything I could to make this company a success, and
> now they're saying that's not enough—that I have to
> "make nice" with the people I work with. I can't believe
> they're coming after me like this—that they're treating
> me this way.
>
> *Coach:* I'm going to challenge you on your belief that this
> is an attack—I don't think that's an accurate reading of

the situation. If your company wanted to attack you, they could have done it by firing or demoting you or finding some other way to take you out of the picture. They've done the exact opposite. They obviously want you here, or they wouldn't have gone to the effort of confronting you on your abrasive behavior and giving you an opportunity to turn things around. Let me tell you, I'm not sitting in this chair for free—the fact that your employer is willing to pay for coaching tells me that management wants to invest in you.

Abrasive Boss: Maybe, maybe not—I don't' know what to make of this.

Coach: There's something else I want you to be aware of. I think your managers are doing you a big favor by bringing their concerns to your attention and offering help. As a corporate executive and executive coach, I've experienced the cultures of hundreds of companies. Let me tell you—there's a very high probability that your current management style would be considered unacceptable wherever you decide to continue your career. If you don't get a handle on the issues here, they're going to plague you in the future.

Abrasive Boss: I don't know—I need to think about it.

The Case for Early Intervention

All too often I'm called in when the situation has reached crisis proportions. Having given free rein to abrasive bosses to trample their coworkers, these companies now face threats presented by the employees who've been seared with their boss's aggressive brand. These working wounded are ready to defend themselves through fight (litigation) or flight (bolting to another company)—defenses that threaten the organization's fitness. There's no reason to let the situation deteriorate to this point, because early intervention has a greater chance of success.

As soon as you detect a pattern of abrasive behavior, set the limit and hold the individual accountable for interacting respectfully with fellow employees. Early detection allows for early intervention: it's easier to mentor bosses when they're only irritating, before they (d)evolve into *Bossus abrasivus*.

Congratulations—you've done your best to make the abrasive boss see the harm he or she does and care enough to want to change. You've invoked the survival dynamic by threatening the costs of continued abrasion, and you've done it in a respectful manner. But before we discover if the boss will drink from the well of change, we need to consider the very risky business of handling an abrasive boss you work *for*—boss whispering from below.

11

Risky Business

Taming the Boss You Work for or with

This chapter is written for those who work for or with an abrasive boss—you who work on the same rung as the boss or labor lower on the corporate ladder. I've grouped you together because, even though you may be at different levels, you share one thing in common—*neither of you has any authority over the abrasive boss who is making your life a misery.* Like the abrasive boss's superiors, if you want to see any hope of change, you're going to have to do some boss taming—you're going to have to do your best to make your abrasive boss see and care about the suffering you've experienced from his or her harsh words and actions. You're going to have to take the blinders off and put the limits on without the benefit of authority. This chapter will show you how, based on the paces that I've seen insightful coworkers put their emotionally blind bosses *and* companies through. Trust me—any doubters can look this gift horse in the mouth because I didn't think these up. You're not looking at a consultant's confabulations. These strategies came straight from the mouths and actions of employees who successfully tamed their abrasive bosses—employees who bravely blazed trails that put a stop to their suffering.

Perhaps this isn't the first book you've read on this topic—you may already have surveyed the "survival guides" that describe elaborate strategies to outlast, outwit, or outplay your abrasive boss. In accordance with the survival dynamic, these strategies fall into the defense categories of fight or flight. The primary flight strategy (*duck and cover*) advises you to bear the unbearable by letting the stress caused by your abrasive boss roll off you like—you guessed it—water off a duck's back. No kidding—one author urges you to make like a duck who "shakes itself off from time to time and goes about its business," not allowing the boss to "dampen" your spirit. Gack (or should I say *quack*). Sitting ducks are also encouraged to exercise, visualize calmer ponds, and breathe deeply to manage their stress. Supposedly, by taking flight into whatever refuge you decide on, you will *outlast* the malaise of the moment to live another day in misery. And if you paddle through your pain long enough, you could metamorphose from lame duck to lucky duck, outlasting your abrasive boss, who has moved on to bigger and better ponds.

If flight strategies don't suit your fancy, there's always the defense option—you can fight. *Outwit* strategies call for deceptive ducks to trick their abrasive bosses with endless psychological gambits designed to keep bosses at bay. Such tactics can be risky, exhausting, and worst of all, ineffective. I've encountered more than one crispy duck who was roasted in the retaliatory fire of an abrasive boss who detected the employee's deceit. Then there's the *outplay* strategy, in which you are encouraged to flex your mighty duck muscles and engage in direct combat against further abrasion by reporting your boss to higher authorities. Let me tell you—there's no faster route to ending up a dead duck than this one. Higher authorities, namely, management and human resource types, don't like to deal with messy personnel problems, otherwise known as *duck poop*. If you embark on the outplay strategy without knowing how to navigate these waters, chances are very good that you, dear duck, will get *shot right out of the water—purged from the pond.*

This boss whisperer is a straight shooter, so here goes: frankly, I don't give a damn for these strategies. I've rarely seen them have any positive effect, much less restore a wounded workplace to health. I believe that people should have the right to go to work without being subjected to aggression, but if you want to spend your working life mired in misery, engaged in wearisome battles of wit or just waiting for your boss (or you) to croak, that's your choice. If you listen to these authors, they'll tell you that your choices are limited: futile fighting, duck and cover freezing, or fleeing the scene entirely. I'm feeling my abrasive oats as I disrespectfully disagree with these authors, because I've come across a few odd ducks who flew different routes—who blazed effective strategies to tame the abrasive bosses they worked for or with. I'm going to share those strategies with you, but before I do that, I'd like to set the stage with another tale of wilderness survival.

Arctic Anxiety

On those occasions when I'm challenged on my ability to stand my ground with an abrasive boss, I can't restrain the impulse to boast: "After standing down a grizzly bear, standing my ground with an abrasive boss is a piece of cake." You can't accuse me of being abrasive—just obnoxious. Intrigued? Here's the Hollywood version, in case anyone is considering the film rights to this book:

Striding through the spruce forest beside a salmon-stuffed river on Alaska's Katmai Peninsula, I came face to face with a grizzly bear. We stopped cold in our tracks—each taken off guard. The bear rose on up on his hind legs to his full height, glared at me, and then slammed his front paws to the ground in a threat display. I stood my ground and stared him down: seeing my steely resolve, he turned and fled.

Here's the real-world version—what *really* happened:

Shuffling through the spruce forest beside a salmon-stuffed river on Alaska's Katmai Peninsula, I came face to face with a grizzly bear. We stopped cold in our tracks—actually, *cold* doesn't quite describe it—I was *frozen*, frozen in fear. The survival dynamic had kicked in—perceiving a threat, I felt fear, but instead of opting for the standard fight or flight options, I instantaneously added another selection to the defense menu: *freeze*. Fight, flee, or freeze. My body was frozen, as was my gaze into the bear's eyes. Here's the important part: *the bear froze too.*

A veritable preteen, still unwise to the ways of his world, he clearly had never encountered the likes of me. And like me, *he* perceived a threat, felt fear, and froze. Our eyes were locked, each paralyzed by the presence of the other. Finally, after I don't know how long, he rose up on his hind legs and then slammed his paws to the ground in a threat display. This did nothing to defrost me: I remained petrified. He turned and fled.

Even in that moment I knew why he made the threat display: *he wanted me to know who was boss.* I also knew why he hotfooted it out of there right after making his display: *he was too afraid to prove he was boss*—he was too afraid to actually use aggression to dominate me. I offer this experience as a lesson in handling abrasive bosses. As I noted in an earlier chapter, bears just want to go about the business of survival—they won't hurt you unless you get in their way. I got in this bear's way, but instead of promptly attacking me, he misinterpreted my glaciated gaze as a threat display—a strategy designed to intimidate him into backing off. To him, *I was the threat.* Without being aware of it, I had succeeded in threatening him, (*gulp*), and because he was insecure about his ability to defend against this unknown threat, *he backed off.*

Defense Disclaimer

If you're working for or with a severely abrasive boss, chances are that you, too, are frozen—frozen in fear. You haven't yet opted to flee to another department or company, nor have you decided to fight for your right to come to work without suffering attack. I have observed employees defrost from their frozen states to take the blinders off their abrasive bosses and make them care about the fact that they attack. But before I describe the various ways to threaten your abrasive boss into adequate behavior, I want to make a very important point: *standing your ground with bears or abrasive bosses is risky business.* With bears you are putting your physical life at great risk; with abrasive bosses you are putting your professional life at great risk. And here's a second critical point: *there are no guarantees*—defending yourself doesn't guarantee that you'll survive to tell the tale.

Before you decide to fight back, I strongly encourage you to consider the alternative defense option: flight. Many members of the animal kingdom would tell you (if they could) that flight is a very effective strategy for avoiding injury. Think about it carefully—do your own cost-benefit analysis of the flight option. How do the costs of sticking around weigh out against the benefits of escaping the threat of further harm through transfer or termination? To answer this question accurately, I recommend that you research other work habitats—lift your nose from the grindstone and look around for other employment opportunities that won't drain the lifeblood from you. Now is the time to get your ducks in a row: buff up your résumé, brush up your networking skills, beef up your savings, and scout new territories. If you decide to take flight, these advance tactics will increase your chances of future survival. And the same holds true if you decide to fight and (unfortunately) *lose*—you'll have a jump start on surviving long enough to locate happier hunting grounds.

Let's say you've completed your cost-benefit analysis of your job, and you've decided it's worth standing your ground for. Fine—keep reading. And for those of you who have decided to flee through transfer or termination, fine—but *keep reading*. Why? Because you are basing your flight plan on one mammoth assumption—that if you fight against abrasion, you're doomed to lose. Assumptions are sheer speculations, otherwise known to scientists as *hypotheses*. We mere mortals call them *guesses*— unfounded estimates of fact. Consider the cost of finding out whether your assumption is founded in fact: what, exactly, have you got to lose if you linger long enough to launch one of the following fight strategies? What price would you pay for testing your hypothesis? I'm not denying that there could be costs attached to the fight option: withheld words or letters of recommendation, blanched benefits, or bad feelings—who knows? But consider the benefit of standing your ground: *you won't spend the rest of your life wondering if there was something you could have done to handle the situation.* You'll have peace of mind, knowing that you did everything in your admittedly limited power to turn the abrasive boss around and make him or her care enough to want to change.

Five Strategies for Subordinates and Peers

In the course of my ramblings I encountered five strategies that halted the harm done by abrasive bosses: the *Soothe Strategy*, the *Reverse Threat Display*, the *Abrasion Alert*, the *Abrasion Alarm*, and the *Mass Mutiny*. However, only the first two strategies (the Soothe Strategy and the Reverse Threat Display) are applied directly to the abrasive boss—the remaining three are applied to your organization's management—those with the authority to manage the unmanageable. Like horse whisperers, you're going to attempt to rein in a highly anxious individual—in your case, your abrasive boss. And if you don't succeed, you're going to climb up the chain of command and do your best to spur management into taming him or her.

Most of the following five strategies are variations on the survival dynamic theme: threat → fear → defense. With the exception of the Soothe Strategy, you're going to trigger this survival dynamic with your abrasive boss or, if necessary, on avoidant management. In short, you're going to do your best to make *them* see and care by taking their blinders off and putting limits on. Once you've opened their eyes, you're going to present *your* threat against continued abrasion—you're going to stand your ground and respectfully intimidate them into treating you with respect. I have to warn you, though: these strategies are doomed to failure if you show fear or anger. I'm alive today because I stared the bear down and stayed silent. I absolutely believe that any displays of fear (wild eyes) or aggression (growls) on my part would have sealed my fate—between the bear's jaws. Before you enter the corporate corral to tame an abrasive boss, heed these whispered words: *never, ever let them see the whites of your eyes or hear the fear in your heart.*

You're going to present your threat, but you need to do it calmly and quietly, much like the concerned physician who advises his patients of looming medical threats. Because I'm whispering, you may have missed that: *calmly* and *quietly*. There's no room for raised voices or aggressive gestures. They will only provoke your boss into aggression. No, you want to gently whisper the costs of continued aggression, *without being aggressive.* Your objective: to quietly escalate your boss's anxiety to the point where he or she abandons (flees) aggressive behavior in favor of a kinder, gentler management style.

Looking calm and speaking quietly may require you to brush up on your acting skills. I don't expect you to *feel* cool, calm, and collected, but you'd better *act* that way—this is one moment when brute honesty will only result in your being brutalized. I'm serious about the whites of your eyes part—recent research reveals that the sight of fear-widened eyes triggers chemical reactions in the amygdala, the primitive brain center responsible for fight or flight reactions (Whalen et al., 2004). You don't want your boss to see your fear or hear your anger, thereby agitating the boss's amygdala, so you may have to *act* what you don't *feel.* Actors rehearse their parts before taking the stage, and I encourage you to rehearse your role repeatedly before you stand your ground. Role-play with people who've observed abrasive bosses and ask them to run through worst-case conversational scenarios with you. Do not, I repeat, *do not* think of standing your ground until you've reached the point where you can, like the very best horse (or patient or kid) whisperers, convey your threat in a concerned, composed manner.

The Soothe Strategy

Many say *music soothes the savage beast,* and I say *reassurance can* (sometimes) *soothe the anxious boss.* This is the only strategy where you won't be presenting a threat: instead of escalating your abrasive boss's anxiety over incompetence, in the Soothe Strategy you'll be working to reduce or eliminate the possibility that he or she will perceive you as a threat. I hope this book has removed blinders from your eyes: you now see that abrasive bosses resort to aggression to eliminate any perceived obstacles to their quest for supercompetence. If you have the misfortune to be perceived as one of those obstacles, you're going to feel the pain. Let's analyze a typical scenario: strolling down the hallway to a meeting, you turn a corner and come face to face with *Bossus abrasivus.*

> *Abrasive Boss:* Where are we on those numbers? I can't move ahead until we know how much this whole project is going to cost.
>
> *You:* I don't have them yet—I—
>
> *Abrasive Boss (cutting in):* What do you mean you "don't have them yet"?! Don't you realize that this is going to delay the whole project? Don't you understand how important this is!? [Inference of stupidity.] How could you let this happen—why didn't you get on this sooner? [Inference of sloth.] What do I have to do to get you to wake up and care enough to do the job?! [Accusation of apathy.] I can see that I'm going to have to do something about this. [Threat display.]
>
> *You* freeze in your tracks.
>
> *Abrasive Boss* storms off, contemplating your imminent extinction.

In the blind eyes of your boss, you've committed the capital crime of incompetence. In that moment he perceives you as a threat to his professional supercompetence. Provoked into a state of high anxiety (you may see the whites of *his* eyes at this point), he defends against the terrifying psychological threat of incompetence by projecting the whole mess onto you: *plop.*

Your boss has leapt to the assumption that you don't care as much about competence as he does because you're lazy, stupid, or uncaring, or all three. *You want to stop this thinking in its tracks.* You need to kill off this misperception before it lives to torment you another day, and *you're going to kill it with kindness.* You're going to dispel this destructive distortion by whispering reassurances of your commitment to competence, his *and* yours. Here's an example from an individual who, having defrosted from his frozen state of fear, returned to soothe his anxious boss and calmly combat these pernicious misperceptions:

> *Employee:* Could I talk with you for a moment?
>
> *Abrasive Boss:* Yes, but I don't have long.
>
> *Employee:* Thanks—I wanted to go back to what happened in the hallway this morning. When you asked me for the numbers on the project estimate, I told you that I didn't have them yet. You got pretty worked up and cut me off before I could finish. I can see how my response set you off—I'd be bothered if that's all I got from one of my guys. [Exercise of empathy.] But if I'd been able to finish my sentence, you would have heard that even though I didn't have them then, I'd gotten a commitment from Accounting to have them on my desk by noon—here they are.
>
> *Abrasive Boss:* Oh—OK.
>
> *Employee:* Nate, you need to know that I care as much about this project as you do. I'm here to make it happen and make us look good in the process. [I'm caring.] I've been all over it, and I'm going to stay all over it. [I'm competent.] You don't have to worry about my support. [I'm committed.] Here's the thing—if you sense that things are going out of control, it would work a lot better if you'd hang in there to talk about it instead of cutting me off. [Teaching moment.] That's all I wanted to say—thanks.
>
> *Abrasive Boss:* Yeah—OK.

The next time you're subjected to your abrasive boss's aggression, consider these steps of the Soothe Strategy:

1. Describe the attack in neutral terms. (*Blinders off.*)
2. Acknowledge your boss's anxiety over incompetence. (*Empathy on.*)
3. Reassure your boss of *his* or *her* competence. (*Soothe.*)
4. Reassure your boss of *your* competence. (*Soothe.*)
5. Teach your boss new ways to manage his or her anxiety without attacking. (*Low-pitched limits on.*)

Remember, you're about to come face to face with an anxious individual, and you'll want to do everything in your power to keep the fur from flying. Wait until you've calmed yourself down to the point where you can *act* with deference and respect toward the boss, even if you don't *feel* it. Here's another example of calmly offering reassurances to soothe the anxious boss:

Employee: Do you have a minute?

Abrasive Boss: Yeah, I guess. What do you want?

Employee: I wanted to clear up something that happened in today's meeting. When I asked you why we're holding off on starting up the new division, you reacted pretty strongly. [Neutral description of attack.] In retrospect, I wonder if you thought I was digging my heels in on the whole thing. [Exercise of empathy.] That's not the case at all—I'm fine with whatever date you set, [Reassurance of boss's dominance.] but it will help me to deal with the press if I know what drove the decision. [Reassurance of employee's competence.]

Abrasive Boss: You're right—I thought you were challenging me. [Confession of perception of threat.]

Employee: Look, Hal, you know what you're doing—I know that. [Reassurance of boss's competence.] And I also want you to know that I'm not here to get in your way—I'm here to get everyone to get *out* of the way so we can move ahead. [Reassurance of employee's motivation.] From now on, if you have any questions about why I'm doing what I'm doing, don't hesitate to ask me directly—I don't want you to waste time worrying about where I'm coming from. [Teaching moment.]

That's the Soothe Strategy—short, relatively sweet, and not always entirely sincere. These employees empathically removed their bosses' blinders and used low tones to set limits on boss aggression by offering alternatives to attack. They took a calm, collegial approach to handling their boss's anxiety, whispering reassurances designed to soothe the anxious boss. As I noted earlier, I can't guarantee that this strategy will work the first time—or at all. Don't expect miracles: repeat application of the soothing treatment as needed, and you may see improvement. However, if your reassurances fail to reduce your boss's anxiety, consider the only other treatment formulated for direct application to abrasive bosses: a dose of their own medicine—*threat*.

The Reverse Threat Display

This defense strategy takes you one step higher on the scale of risk. You're going to do unto your boss as he or she has done unto you—you're going to quietly threaten your boss into abandoning his or her abrasive behavior. I have seen this work, but it takes a lot of courage and the ability to act confidently even if you're shaking in your shoes. Here's how it works: *Bossus abrasivus* has just made an aggressive display intended to intimidate you into competence. He's done this in the belief that his threat display will mobilize you into doing what he wants you to do. You, to his surprise, will stand your ground and respond with a threat of your own to intimidate him into doing what *you* want *him* to do: *back off*.

I first learned about this strategy from coworkers of the courageous employees who successfully blocked their bosses' attacks:

> "He treats everybody like that . . . except for Linda—he doesn't pull that crap with her. He did at first, but then one day she just stood up to him. She just told him she wasn't going to put up with that kind of treatment. For some reason he backed off—he didn't go after her after she did that."

> "I don't know why, but she never does her thing with Daniel. She'll rip into everyone but him. I don't get it. They're not exactly buddies—he can't stand her."

I didn't pay much attention to reports of this strategy until I sat with the individuals who'd actually used the Reverse Threat Display:

> "I told him that he didn't need to talk to me that way, and that I wouldn't tolerate it."

> "I told her that I don't appreciate being treated badly and that when people do that to me, it has the reverse effect. She never did it again."

> "I told him my father used to yell at me as a kid and that I refuse to put up with it as an adult. He still yells, but not at me."

It was clear that all of these threat-slingers were determined to set limits on their bosses' abrasive behavior, reminiscent of the gunslinger played by John Wayne in *The Shootist*: "*I won't be wronged, I won't be insulted, and I won't be laid a hand on. I don't do these things to other people and I require the same from them.*" It was also clear that these employees presented their threats in cool, collected tones, in accordance with the Duke's advice to actors: "*Talk low, talk slow, and don't talk too much.*"

The employees I spoke with applied two variations of the Reverse Threat Display: *veiled* and *defined*. In the Veiled Reverse Threat Display no reference was made to how the employee intended to make good on the threat. In the Defined Reverse Threat Display employees specified the next step they'd take if the boss didn't back off and behave appropriately. I present the condensed versions:

Veiled Reverse Threat Display: "I told him that I wouldn't tolerate it any more."

Defined Reverse Threat Display: "I told her that if she kept it up, I'd be forced to take it to HR or further up the chain."

The veiled display is likely to provoke less defensiveness, because even though on the one hand you're presenting a threat, on the other hand you're giving your boss the opportunity to harness his or her aggressive impulses. Don't use this strategy without acquainting yourself with the defensive maneuvers discussed in Chapters Nine and Ten. Avoid crippling fact battles by presenting your feelings as fact: "*You* may think that what you said in the meeting wasn't humiliating but *I felt* deeply offended." Disarm your boss's defenses with the same strategies I recommended for managers of abrasive bosses, as in the following variations on the defense-disarming Veiled Reverse Threat Display.

The "That's Not What Happened" Denial

Abrasive Boss: That's not what happened—you're blowing it all out of proportion. You're making a big deal out of nothing.

Employee: I don't want to debate what happened. What I do know is the way you treated me today was way out of line, and I want it to stop. You don't need to act like that to get me to do what you want.

The "It's Your Fault" Projection

Abrasive Boss: When you pushed back, it really pushed my buttons.

Employee: I wasn't trying to challenge you—I was just asking for clarification. I had no idea you'd see my question as a challenge. I just want to figure out how to pull all of this off without setting *you* off. I'm not into public floggings—next time, just ask.

The "It's Necessary" Rationalization

Abrasive Boss: Sometimes I have to get on your case to get things moving.

Employee: You may see it that way, but I don't. I work very hard to move things along, and if I'm delayed because other departments haven't responded, I don't appreciate your taking it out on me. If yelling at me is the only way you think you can get things moving, you're wrong—it doesn't help. If you have concerns, bring them to me without yelling. I won't tolerate being treated that way anymore.

Remember to look and sound calm and collected, even if a storm of anger rages within. This is *absolutely essential*—you want your boss to see your logic, not your rage. Displays of intense emotion will distract attention from your case and give the boss a welcome excuse to escalate into lethal aggression to avoid dealing with your feedback. You don't want to provoke a bloody dominance struggle. You're more than willing to submit to the top dog's authority, but only if he stops chewing on you.

Here's the prescription for the Soothe and Reverse Threat Display strategies:

1. In cases of boss abrasion, apply the Soothe Strategy directly to the boss. If improvement is noted, continue application of soothing reassurance until abrasive behavior disappears.

2. If no improvement is noted after a minimum of three applications of the Soothe Strategy, apply the Veiled Reverse Threat Display, injecting a direct threat only if the veiled threat fails to yield results. Either display may be rendered more palatable when prefaced with the Soothe Strategy (remember—a spoonful of sugar helps the medicine go down). Caution: administering either of these threats, veiled or direct, may jeopardize your career health. Displays of strong emotion are contraindicated.

There you have it: the two strategies that I've seen work when applied directly to the boss. If they haven't yielded results, you've now reached the end of your boss-taming rope, because, realistically, you don't have the authority to set stronger limits on your boss. You can *ask* bosses to back off, but you can't demand it, which leads us to your only remaining alternative: threatening those who have the authority to set limits on the abrasive boss into doing exactly that. You're going to change horses midstream by shifting the threat of the abrasive boss from *you* to *your company*—you're going to make management feel the threat of failing to intervene with the abrasive boss.

The Abrasion Alert: Making Management See

The Abrasion Alert consists of calmly and respectfully informing organizational authorities of the potential threat they face if they don't address the abrasive boss's behavior. In this approach you make *your* problem with your boss's behavior *their* problem. You'll do this by presenting them with your version of the survival dynamic: *threat* of noxious employee reaction to abrasion → *fear* of work disruption → *defensive* intervention with abrasive boss. Because your attempts to leash top dog have failed, you're going to pass the anxiety to someone with a leash.

Management (and I include human resource staff in this group) may or may not be aware of the presence of abrasion. In either case your first task is to take *their* blinders off—to ensure they see what's going on. I start with an example of a bungled approach to the Abrasion Alert strategy, an approach used by too many distressed employees that should be avoided at all costs:

> *Manager (HR or otherwise):* What's up?
>
> *Employee (in loud, agitated tones):* I want to talk to you about something that happened today—I'm so angry I can barely talk. We were in a production meeting and Chris started going after me. I can't stand that guy—he is such a jerk.
>
> *Manager:* What do you mean?
>
> *Employee:* I was telling him that we need to run more trials on the new platform before we release it. Next thing I know he's drilling me with all of these questions: *"Haven't you taken care of that already? Why am I hearing about this now?!"* He just ripped into me, right in front of everyone. He even called me "stupid"—I know he's had it in for me for a long time.
>
> *Manager:* What do you mean, "ripped into you"?
>
> *Employee:* You know—his usual temper tantrum. He can be such a big baby—you guys should fire him. So what exactly are you going to do about this?

We might better term this particular intervention the *suicide strategy,* for without being aware of it, you will succeed only in cutting your own throat with this approach. I've seen this strategy played out innumerable times, all with the same negative results:

- You will be perceived as irrational and abrasive because of your highly emotional and disrespectful descriptions of your boss.

- You may be suspected of "having it in for your boss," thereby eradicating any hope that your complaint will be considered valid and worthy of management's attention.

- You will come across as demanding and abrasive toward the manager or HR staff person, motivating him or her to terminate the conversation as soon as politically possible.

- The manager will mention your meeting to your abrasive boss, describing it along these lines: "Arnold showed up in my office today with some complaint about how you got on his case—what's going on between you two?" Your abrasive boss will speedily convince the manager that you are a difficult case, mentioning your complaint about your last raise for extra effect. The manager will be thoroughly convinced that you're a difficult duck, having already personally experienced a difficult meeting with "difficult" you. (*Final Score: Abrasive Boss, 1; Manager, 1; Duck, dead.*)

Get my drift? So when you finally screw up the courage to bite the bullet and make your case, don't screw it up with any unpleasant, alienating, and yes, *abrasive* behavior from your end. You want to be perceived as rational, reasonable, concerned, and most of all, *helpful*. It won't hurt to exercise a little empathy for management in this situation: how would you feel if you were a member of management listening to someone quack on and on about how a boss ruffled his or her feathers, followed by a demand that you do something—*right now*? You want to motivate your company into action with carrots, not sticks, because *abrasion provokes defense*. Earlier in this book I described how abrasive bosses are eventually plagued with negative perceptions of their behavior, surrounded by harmful perceptual horseflies that follow them everywhere. You don't want any horseflies hovering over you as you alert your organization to the presence of an abrasive boss. You don't want them buzzing that you're lazy, stupid, or vindictive. Such perceptions, however inaccurate, will weaken your case and kill off any hope of being heard. To make your case you'll have to avoid any chance of being misperceived as a troublemaker, whiner, or difficult type. Remember, you can't help but be perceived as a threat the moment you bring your concern to management. Your objective is to change that perception from *threat* to *rescue*—to make management see that you're there not to harm the company but to help rescue it from a terrible fate. Here's the strategy in action with a human resource manager:

> *You:* Is this still a good time to meet?
>
> *HR Manager:* Absolutely—come on in. What's up?
>
> *You:* Leo, I don't want to take a lot of your time, but there's a situation that I think you should be aware of. I debated about coming to you, but I decided that you'd want to know.
>
> *HR Manager:* What's going on?
>
> *You:* Leo, you know that Max was brought in from the Eastern Division to run our department. He's got a lot going for him—he's very intelligent, sizes things up quickly, and from what I can see, he's made some very good decisions. The problem is that he's alienating a lot of people, including me. I can't speak for the others, but I've found him very difficult to work with because he gets very aggressive for no reason. For instance, if someone asks him a question, he immediately perceives it as a challenge and cuts them off. This morning I asked him when we'd start up the next phase, and he barked, "Get off my back—don't you think I know what I'm doing?!" Last week when he got frustrated he called a female employee an "idiot"—he hasn't tried that yet with me. I've heard of two people who are actively searching for new jobs, and I know that even though he's well-intentioned, people aren't going to put up with this forever [*veiled threat*].
>
> *HR Manager:* What do you want me to do about it?
>
> *You:* I don't know—that's why I brought it to you. I just wanted you to be aware of what's going on.

That's it—the Abrasion Alert strategy in action. No anger, no demands, no overt threats. But wait—*are you calling me a softy?* Do these grains of wisdom seem a bit mealymouthed? Are you attacking my logic? If so, it's time for me to get defensive, otherwise known as presenting my superior reasoning:

- Your demeanor is one of concern and composure—no spooked sclera here. Your soothing presence invites attention. Leo *wants* to hear what you have to say. (*Defenses decrease.*)

- You open by recognizing the abrasive boss's considerable strengths, which attests to your good judgment and positive regard for the company's decision to bring him in (*reassurance of your competence*). Leo's feeling better and better about you—you're a company man (or woman). (*Defenses drop even further.*)

- You present the specific abrasive behaviors inflicted on you and others. You make Leo see. (*Blinders come off.*)

- You allude to the possibility of sexual harassment toward a female employee. (*First threat is presented.*)

- You refer to employees preparing to jump ship. (*Second threat is presented.*)

- You hint that you aren't going to tolerate the abrasion. (*Third threat is presented.*)

Notice that you've kept the focus on the abrasive boss—not on you. You've got Leo thinking about Max—not about you. You've presented threats and escalated the company's anxiety about Max—*not about you.* By the way, if you're harboring hopes of simply strolling in and laying your cards on the table only to have your abrasive boss face a firing squad, forget it. The company has a major investment in your boss and a further investment in maintaining the status quo. From the company's perspective, he or she may be doing a lot that's right. Your abrasive boss may be hitting high numbers, cutting costs, or keeping production on an even keel.

Let's get real—here's what you should reasonably expect. First, you want the company to be aware of the situation and then set limits on it. Second, you want your company to hold your boss accountable for interpersonal competence and require him or her to relinquish aggressive management tactics. These are not unreasonable demands. You're not asking for any special favors or calling for your boss's head—two actions that companies are reluctant to take. You are simply asking to be treated in a nonhostile (also known as *respectful*) manner. You're not dictating demands—you're respectfully asking to be freed from harassment so that you can do your job unencumbered by emotional distress. Issuing demands puts management on the defensive, shifting the perception of threat back to you. Instead, limit yourself to a calm, clear presentation of your concerns and let management worry about how they're going to deal with your boss. Here are some defense-reducing elaborations of the Abrasion Alert strategy:

- *Empathize with the pressures facing your boss and your company:* "I know Max is facing major deadlines and that we're under the gun."

- *Emphasize your commitment to the organization:* "You know, I've worked here for eighteen years, and I really believe in this company. That's why I came to you—I can't believe it's good for the company to have Max treating people that way."

- *Describe what you've done to try to solve the problem:* "I've talked with him twice to try and make him see how he's alienating the people he needs most, but he just doesn't see it."

- *Empathize with management's dilemma:* "I don't know if someone can get through to him. It's really a shame, because he is so incredibly intelligent and motivated."

There's one more thing to remember when you consider the Abrasion Alert strategy: refrain from any temptation to specify how your company should intervene with the abrasive boss. In the last example the HR representative asked, "What do you want me to do about it?" Don't fall into the trap of telling management what to do. Realistically, *that's none of your business*—it's their business, and don't get in the way of it. There's no law, however, against hypnotic management whispering: *"Gee, I don't know what would help. Maybe you guys talking to him or some coaching—I don't really know."* But don't fall into the trap of taking an authoritative stance where you have no authority.

There—you've done it—you've taken your best shot at making management see. You've done everything in your very limited power to open management's eyes by respectfully presenting the threat of abrasion. Even better, you did it with emotional intelligence, intentionally escalating management anxiety without allowing that anxiety to ricochet back on you. *Good shot.* But don't expect miracles after the first alert—further alerts may be needed to build your case. Patience can pay. Also, don't forget that there's strength in numbers, so consider the advantages of the *Serial Abrasion Alert.* In this variation, other wounded coworkers follow your example and calmly sound *their* alerts to management, using the tactics just described.

The Abrasion Alarm: Making Management Care

If the Abrasion Alert strategy fails to yield results, you can take the next step up the risk scale. Let me warn you: this is a major step in which you not only take the corporate bull by the horns—you're going to wave the red flag of threat right in its eyes. In the course of my work I've had many opportunities to observe human resource staff going about their business. From my conversations with employees who stood up to abrasion, I learned of four corporate jungle calls that—*without fail*—make HR types sit up and take notice: *hostile environment, harassment, discrimination,* and *legal action.* But unlike chest-pummeling apes who charge about in wild threats of aggression, these employees took a more subtle approach: they simply invoked one of these four phrases in a very quiet (and seemingly nonthreatening) way:

> "This is starting to feel like a *hostile environment.*"
>
> "Is this what they call *harassment?*"
>
> "Isn't picking on a person of another sex [or race, ethnicity, or era] a form of *discrimination?*"
>
> "I can see why people would bring *legal action* if they were being treated this way."

The effects of these oblique threats can be immediate—the alarm bells start ringing, and so does my telephone: "We've got a potentially serious situation we need help with—are you available?" Time and time again I'm called in after management has gotten wind of potential legal action. Threats of legal action, however indirect, send chills spiraling down the spines of spineless managers—bosses who've fled the challenge of handling an abrasive boss. Such legal actions can be messy and expose a company to major threats of annihilation (through monetary loss) and abandonment (through loss of reputation). If you want to fly the most threatening flag, this is the one.

Don't get me wrong: *I am not*—repeat *not*—*encouraging you to sue your employer.* Under most circumstances I'd advise against this, the *All-Out Attack* strategy, for many reasons. Some of the greatest words of wisdom were written on my *tabula rasa* by a lawyer friend who advised me to avoid legal recourse if at all possible, "because the minute you turn your matter over to a court, you lose control. The *court* will control your fate—*not you.*" Think about it. Do you really want to ruin more years of your life—financially and otherwise—tied up in legal action that could very possibly fizzle into failure? (Corporations, like kangaroos, have very deep pockets.) If the situation has become intolerable, do you want to subject yourself to further distress by pursuing litigation? And there's something else you should be aware of before you rush to court: in the United States, *there's no law against abrasion*. It's not illegal to be abrasive unless a boss specifically targets employees because of their sex, race, religion, national origin, age, or disability. If an abrasive boss attacks older employees to get them to resign, you're looking at age discrimination. But if an abrasive boss indiscriminately attacks *anyone*, old or young, for the same reason, you're looking at lawlessness in the wilds of work.

How risky is the Abrasion Alarm strategy? This is open to debate, but there's no question that executing this strategy transforms you into a force to be dealt with. You've made a potent threat display, and from this point on you will be perceived as a serious threat to the survival of your boss and your company. Paradoxically, applying the Abrasion Alarm strategy may reduce the possibility of retaliation, in that legislation does exist to protect whistle-blowers. But don't let your guard down, because organizations have means other than termination to extinguish threats. If your company takes an adversarial stance against you (instead of advocating for your right to be treated in a civil manner), it can find all sorts of ways to exile you (unwelcome transfer to the Timbuktu division) or starve you out (demotion or excruciatingly dull work assignments).

If you elect to execute the Abrasion Alarm strategy, do so only after you've calculated the risks of execution: *risk only what you can afford to lose*. Do not apply any of these strategies until you've gotten your financial and professional ducks in a row as earlier advised. I also strongly recommend that you consult with an employment attorney to get a realistic calculation of your odds of success and the potential for problems. This is neither the time nor the place to naively act on fantasies of revenge.

Mass Mutiny

There's one final strategy, and it offers two advantages—high yield on investment and little or no individual risk: the Mass

Mutiny. This strategy involves the following steps:

1. Marshal the tormented troops.
2. March to Human Resources.
3. Voice your distress in concert (abrasive tones should be avoided).
4. Respectfully declare, in chorus, some version of "We're sick from being treated this way, and we can't and won't take it anymore."

This may be the most effective strategy for motivating a foot-dragging company to take the abrasive boss by the horns. It consists of multiple employees presenting their concerns en masse to management, with statements to the tune of "This can't go on—we can't go on." It's a bold move, but as many species have discovered, there can be safety in numbers: *united we stand, divided we crawl.* Before you decamp from your department to mutiny, be sure that all participants undergo basic training in calm conduct, communicating concern for the company, and specific substantiation of their charges of abrasion. As with the other strategies there's no guarantee that the Mass Mutiny strategy will produce results. Remember to handle management with care—never engage in direct attack, because, as humorist Kin Hubbard tells us: "*Nobody ever forgets where he buried the hatchet.*"

12

The Choice to Change

Will the Horse Drink?

You can do your best to tame an abrasive boss. Whether manager, subordinate, or peer, you can exercise empathy to read the fears that drive abrasive bosses to aggression, and then do everything in your admittedly limited powers to illuminate their blind spots and hope that they'll care enough to change their wounding ways. You can do your best to make abrasive bosses see the need for change by exerting environmental pressure to change, but will the abrasive boss drink from the well of change?

Who knows? I don't. I can't predict behavior, human or otherwise, and I wouldn't trust any boss whisperer who claimed such psychic powers. Will the horse drink? Will the boss change? Maybe yes—maybe no, but you'll never know unless you do what you can to harness their aggressive styles. As a subordinate or peer, you may strive to soothe the anxious boss's fears of incompetence. Hopefully, that will be all it takes to bring him or her into line—I've seen it work for some, and it may for you. If it doesn't work, you can try to set limits on the boss's behavior with the Reverse Threat Display, presenting a veiled or direct threat of the consequences for continued aggression. I've met employees who used this strategy with success, and you may see a similar positive response. And if these two strategies designed for direct application to the boss don't yield the desired results, you can redirect your taming efforts to management by deploying the Abrasion Alert, Abrasion Alarm, or Mass Mutiny strategies to get your company's higher-ups to take *their* blinders off and see the need to intervene. If managers are willing to drink from the well of change and step up to the task of taming the abrasive boss, there's a chance that you'll not only survive but live on to emotionally thrive in your current work environment.

And as a member of management, you can do your best to disarm defensiveness and make abrasive bosses see the harmful perceptions draining the lifeblood from their competence. You too can threaten consequences for failing to change, and if they choose to change, you can offer help in the form of personal mentoring or expert coaching to help them handle their aggression. But will the horse drink? As I said, I don't know—I can't predict the path your abrasive boss will take, but I *can* predict that it will be one of these four options:

1. Abrasive bosses won't see their abrasive impact and therefore can't change. (*They're unable.*)

2. Abrasive bosses will see their abrasive impact but won't care enough to change. (*They're unwilling.*)

3. Abrasive bosses will see their abrasive impact and will care enough to change and will succeed. (*They're willing and able.*)

4. Abrasive bosses will see their abrasive impact and care enough to change, and will fail. (*They're willing and unable.*)

You've tolerated the abrasion long enough—frozen in fear—but now you've decided to take flight from that paralyzing pond of pain. You're prepared to take bosses by the horns and do your best to make them see and care. And if your efforts to tame abrasive bosses succeed, they will choose to evolve softer spots and coexist with respect for their coworkers. That's path no. 3: you came, they saw, and they cared enough to conquer their aggressive impulses. If abrasive bosses travel any of the other three trails, you're left with only two options: *isolate* or *terminate*. Subordinates can isolate themselves from future pain by transferring out of the abrasive boss's department, and peers can search out ways to stay out of range of the abrasive boss's wrath. Managers can isolate the abrasive boss by putting him or her out to solitary pastures or projects where nobody roams and coworkers will be happy all day. If solitary confinement isn't an option, abrasive bosses who are unable or unwilling to adapt to environmental demands for appropriate conduct should face extinction—the time has come to terminate their survival at your company. Peers and subordinates don't have the option of terminating their boss, but they can terminate their own suffering by moving on to greener pastures.

Insightful boss tamers see that abrasive bosses aren't evil— they're *afraid*. They also see that the key to containing this managerial aggression consists of calming the individual's competence anxieties. Once you've confronted abrasive bosses with the choice to change, they may be able to do it all on their own, or they may require your mentoring or more intensive help from a boss whisperer. In any case, don't abandon hope before you even take up the reins. People can change, and they do. Remember Mark, the "bazooka" boss and his cage-rattling management style? He worked hard to develop carrot-based management strategies and has since gone on to found his own company—complete with contented coworkers. However, don't expect miracles: leopards can change their spots, but they can't change the fact that they're leopards. Some recovering abrasive bosses relapse unless environmental pressures are maintained; others are able to evolve to rudimentary but tolerable levels of interpersonal competence: the noxious *Bossus abrasivus* metamorphoses into the innocuous *Bossus annoying-us*. Bosses who see their abrasive impact, care enough to change, and then fail in their efforts are the saddest cases. I mean that literally—it's very sad to see abrasive bosses who have tried and failed to overcome deep fears instilled in childhood, fears that still reverberate through their adult careers, with ruinous results for all concerned.

In either case—best or worse—you'll have the satisfaction of knowing that you did everything in your power to stop workplace suffering: you gave it your best shot. If the horse doesn't drink and you decide to depart, you won't be wondering if there was something you could have done that you didn't. No matter what happens, you'll have peace of mind, knowing that you stood your ground and spoke up for yourself and your fellow working wounded. You stood up, and because of this, you'll be spared the shame of those who stood by:

> "I feel ashamed that I stood by while one person I have
> good rapport with attacked another employee. I felt
> uncomfortable. . . . What inhibited my speaking up?
> Fear. You start to learn that, working here—we don't
> talk to each other—it's just attack. I thought about
> what I'd say to the person, but I just felt so uncomfort-
> able. I stayed silent. What's going to happen if none of
> us stand up for each other?"

Two Stories

I'd like to tell you two true stories of two abrasive bosses—one a hopeless case and the other a case for hope. I call the first story "The Executive's New Clothes."

Once upon a time an executive coach was summoned to a corporate castle by courtiers from the human resource depart- ment to change their sovereign's abrasive management style. "But does the king wish to change styles?" the coach asked. "Does he even see that his current style is overly aggressive?" The courtiers admitted that the king was blind to this fact but convinced the coach that she had magical powers to make him see: "We told him that you're here to assess everyone's wardrobe, but we're sure that you'll find a way to dress *him* in new and better clothes." Still a whisperer's apprentice, the coach was blinded by the audacity of innocence. "Truly, I must try—for the good of the people of this pained kingdom." The coach then spoke with each of the king's subjects, weaving the threads of their anguished conversations into new clothes, which she presented to the king. "Your Highness, I beg you to quit looking like your fool and instead don clothes better suited to a wise man's leadership style." (Here comes the not-so-happy ending.) The king summarily exiled her from the kingdom, and his despairing subjects toiled on in their torment (he did pay her invoice, however).

That's a true story—*my* tale of woe. There's a moral to this story, a painful lesson learned that I'll pass on to you: *If the abrasive boss rules the company, and chooses not to change, you're doomed.* I share this story of hopelessness because I'm constantly asked about this scenario: if top dog is literally at the top of the company heap and chooses not to change, is there any hope? I don't think so. I suppose one could try to convince a board of directors of the need for change, but boards are generally reluctant to overthrow sovereigns they've selected. I think it's a safe bet to assume that unless you leave, you'll labor on in a dungeon of doom.

Now for a tale of hope; the true story of an abrasive boss who managed to contain his aggression with great success. I speak of America's first and (some believe) greatest chief executive officer: George Washington. Contrary to popular belief, little Georgie did not chop down a cherry tree out of rage. In fact he never even took up the hatchet—that's a myth. He was, however, endowed with an abrasive style that he worked to control for the good of his country. This was no easy feat. As one of Washington's colleagues said, "Thousands have learned to restrain their passions, though few among them had to contend with passions so violent." Thomas Jefferson described Washington's temper as "naturally irritable and high-toned," and "when it broke its bonds, he was most tremendous in his wrath." In the biography *Founding Father*, Richard Brookhiser (1996) wrote that Washington's temper "had its raw edges . . . and when they were incautiously touched, he could become dangerous to those around him." Brookhiser goes on to quote Alexander Hamilton's description of how, after four years of service on Washington's staff, Hamilton suffered humiliation (one of the Big Five indicators of an abrasive boss) at General Washington's hands:

> Washington had just chewed him [Hamilton] out. "Two days ago, the General and I passed each other on the stairs" at headquarters. "He told me he wanted to speak to me. I answered that I would wait upon him immediately." Two minutes later, by Hamilton's own count, "I met him at the head of the stairs where, accosting me in an angry tone, 'Colonel Hamilton,' said he, 'you have kept me waiting at the head of the stairs these ten minutes. I must tell you sir, you treat me with disrespect.' " Hamilton resigned then and there [p. 117].

Washington was also guilty of condescension and overcontrol in his quest for supercompetence: "One of Britain's Indian allies who had been with him 'complained very much' of Washington's behavior: he 'command[ed] Indians as his slaves' and 'would by no means take advice . . . but was always driving them on to fight by his directions' " [p. 116].

"Not surprisingly," writes Richard Norton Smith (1994), "Washington's lifelong need for control expressed itself through a mastery of nearly everyone and everything around him" (p. 7).

Like many abrasive bosses, George Washington had early experiences with annihilation and abandonment anxieties: loss of life and loss of love. His father died when he was only eleven, and love was in short supply from a controlling and intimidating mother. "Of the mother, I was ten times more afraid than of my own parents," said a childhood friend of Washington. Immediately following his father's death, his distant, unaffectionate mother sent him off to live with an older half-brother.

But Brookhiser also describes Washington's continuing efforts to control his aggression in order to achieve his objectives:

> Controlling his anger was a lifelong, and never wholly successful, struggle. He lost his temper in Cabinet meetings, once in Congress,

once—spectacularly—in battle. Still he kept reining it in [1996, p. 5].

Washington had a lot to be angry about over the course of his career: untrained soldiers, incompetent officers, difficult allies, quarrelsome associates (including Jefferson)—to say nothing of his own mistakes, from losing battles to misjudging people: Washington trusted Benedict Arnold—a man of great apparent civility, though little real decency—up to the moment he ran off to the enemy. But if he had gone into uncontrollable rages at every disappointment or disaster, he would have ruined his health, besides ruining his effectiveness as a leader [Brookhiser, 1997, p. 14].

His was not a private struggle—his battle against abrasion was known to many, including his portraitist, Gilbert Stuart:

The pattern of closure in Washington's outbursts suggests a pattern of deliberate control. They ended because he willed them to end. Considering the problems that arose during eight and a half years as Commander in Chief and eight years as President, there must have been many storms which were controlled before they burst out. Virtually every observer who noted Washington's temper also noted the close rein he kept on it—including Washington himself. Henry Lee, a family friend, once told the Washingtons that the painter Stuart said his subject had a temper. Martha Washington exclaimed that Stuart had been out of line to say so. Lee finished the story: Stuart had added that the temper was under "wonderful control." "Mr. Stuart is right," Washington remarked. . . .

Washington's temperament was like the horses he rode [Brookhiser, 1996, p. 119]

Washington did not achieve a perfect victory over his aggressive tendencies—he was human, like the rest of us. But he worked long and hard enough on self-control to achieve greatness:

The measure of Washington's success, despite his lapses, is that we have forgotten that he had a problem. We look at Stuart's glacial image, and a dozen other composed and almost emotionless portraits, from the face on Mount Rushmore to the bust on the quarter, and we assume that that's just the way Washington was. His contemporaries knew better: they saw the composure as an end product, the result of early training and continuous effort [Brookhiser, 1997, p.16].

How did Washington manage to manage himself? He committed himself to a code of conduct, setting an example for all those who choose to campaign against workplace suffering.

13

Ending Unnecessary Roughness

Preventing Workplace Abrasion

At the tender age of sixteen, George Washington committed to a code of conduct composed by French Jesuits in 1595. He copied all 110 of *The Rules of Civility and Decent Behavior in Company and Conversation*, and carried this handwritten list with him throughout his life. Washington managed himself according to these principles, refusing to let his volatile emotions get in the way of the challenging business of founding a nation dedicated to equality and justice for all. Companies unwilling to let abrasion get in the way of business also operate according to their own codes of conduct: boot campers quickly learn about military codes of conduct, right down to the specific words ("Yes, *sir!*") and actions (stand and salute) denoting deference and respect. Physicians take the oath of Hippocrates, committing to *primum non nocere*, to above all do no harm to their patients.

Individuals and organizations alike operate according to codes of conduct, whether or not they're aware of them. As kids we all learned the codes of conduct that would or wouldn't be tolerated in our very first organization, the family: "We don't use that kind of language"; "We always say 'thank you'"; "No hitting!" I struggled with these early lessons, especially in relation to my grandmother, at the age of three declaring, "Grandma—you stupid!" in a fit of frustration. The recipient of this insult deemed my behavior "adorable"; however, my parents immediately intervened to remind me of *their* code of conduct, which outlawed epithets.

Work organizations have their own codes of conduct as well, whether or not they're spelled out in a policy manual. As I noted earlier, abrasion is defined differently in different work cultures, and definitions of respectful conduct also vary depending on the work environment. Although fishmongers favor yelling as an acceptable mode of communicating the impending arrival of a flying frozen fish, librarians would quail at the prospect of bellowing at a colleague—doing so would be a sure sign of disrespect. I've worked in organizations where failure to return a phone call within twenty-four hours was considered a prosecutable crime, and I've worked in others where "just couldn't get around to calling you last week" was deemed perfectly acceptable. Along with individuals and families, companies evolve their own standards of interpersonal interaction, some clearly enunciated, others never voiced but carved into the collective corporate unconscious.

The expression of *professional conduct* may vary by country or culture, but the common definition of such conduct remains constant. *Merriam-Webster's Collegiate Dictionary* (11th edition) defines *professional* as "exhibiting a courteous, conscientious, and generally businesslike behavior in the workplace." And before you put your dictionary away, consider this definition of *businesslike:* "Showing ... characteristics advantageous to or of use in business ... practical; *unemotional*" (*American Heritage Dictionary of the English Language*, 4th edition; emphasis added). Professional conduct is unemotional—purged of emotions that *threaten to get in the way of business.* Air traffic controllers observe a code of professional conduct that calls for communicating with pilots in emotion-free monotones, for the safety of the flying public. Controllers and pilots both understand the value of communicating with composure—wild behavior has no place in the wild blue yonder.

With Respect to Respect

We've looked at the impact of abrasion on organizational functioning and strategies for taming abrasive bosses. I'm not going to subject you to a repeat performance of my lecture on the ethics and costs of tolerating abrasion, calculated in terms of attrition, paralyzed production, legal action, and retaliation (they shoot horses *and* bosses). Workplace abrasion is a form of abuse. We've outlawed child abuse, domestic abuse, and elder abuse and are making slow but steady progress on the animal abuse front. So what will it take to make us take workplace abuse seriously in terms of intervention and prevention? And once we choose that path, what are the steps companies need to take to travel it? I believe it starts with a stated code of conduct requiring respectful treatment of coworkers. Such codes are constructed on the key concept of (quoting Aretha Franklin) "R-E-S-P-E-C-T."

What do we mean by respect? Respect is derived from the Latin *respectus*, literally, the act of looking back, to regard—those Romans saw the importance of taking blinders off and giving regard to those in one's environment. I particularly favor the modern definition set forth in Wikipedia, a free online encyclopedia of the people, written by the people, for the people: "Respect is an attitude of acknowledging the feelings and interests of another party in a relationship, and of treating as consequential for the self the helping or harming of the other. Though most commonly referring to interpersonal relationships, it can be used between animals, groups, and institutions including countries. Respect does not necessarily imply deference, but a respectful attitude rules out unconsidered selfish behavior" (Wikipedia, 2006).

For the purposes of this book, I don't think respect requires elaborate definition—we know it when we see it, and we feel it when we don't. Some believe that animals possess an internal mechanism for sensing earthquakes; I believe that humans come equipped with an internal mechanism for sensing disrespect. This mechanism (otherwise known as a *respectometer*) is capable of sensing the slightest shift in interpersonal forces, from barely detectable it's-your-fault lines to convulsive emotional quakes destabilizing work relationships and production. Some of us ignore our respectometer readings, never having received proper self- or other-directed empathy training, but it is harder for organizations to ignore the effects of emotional upheaval when confronted by collapsing morale, crushed initiative, and catastrophic disruptions to the smooth flow of work. One doesn't have to be at the epicenter to suffer the effects of abrasion: aftershocks can be experienced by families and communities as well. No, there's no need to write a thick manual specifying the elements of disrespectful conduct: we know it when we feel it.

Curing Conduct Disorders: A Prescription

I am continually amazed by the fact that even though many companies have established clear performance standards or specific safety codes, very few have spelled out standards for conduct. Companies that go to great lengths to protect the physical safety of employees at work seem blind to the need to safeguard their psychological safety as well. I'd love to see signs declaring "Respect Pays" hung right alongside the "Safety Pays" placards in factories, or how about posting notices proclaiming "846 Days Since the Last Incident of Disrespect" in company lunchrooms? A boss whisperer can dream. . . .

All right—I'm back to reality and ready to give you a prescription for preventing workplace abrasion:

1. Develop a code of conduct.
2. Communicate the code.
3. Live the code.
4. Enforce the code.

A lot of work can go into researching, developing, and implementing codes of conduct. I want to remind you that I'm in the business of developing executive insight—not the business of developing corporate oversight of conduct. I'll be the first to tell you that I don't know everything there is to know about that business, but from my years of roaming a range of organizations as a boss whisperer I've come across a few do's and don'ts that I hope you'll find helpful. Let's take each of the four steps individually.

Develop a Code of Conduct

There's a lot of material out there on writing codes of conduct, and I suppose I could insist that the services of a highly qualified consultant are required to do it properly. But, like George Washington, I cannot tell a lie. Because of this, I'm forced to forgo this opportunity to charge outrageous consulting fees and will instead confess that you can do it all on your own. The key is to *keep it simple* (if I were abrasive, I'd add "*stupid*," but I'm not). If you look at global codes of interpersonal conduct (of which there are very few), you'll see that they too are strikingly simple. I offer three examples, starting with Bill Clinton's "No Sweat" initiative to end abusive treatment of garment industry sweatshop employees (including children) worldwide, better known as the Apparel Industry Partnership Workplace Code of Conduct and Principles of Monitoring:

> Every employee shall be treated with respect and dignity. No employee shall be subject to any physical, sexual, psychological or verbal harassment or abuse" [Williams, 2000, p. 353].

Here's a second example, excerpted from the Caux Principles, created by an international group of business executives who believe that the world business community should strive to improve global economic and social conditions:

> We believe in the dignity of every employee and we therefore have a responsibility . . . to provide working conditions that respect employees' health and dignity [Williams, 2000, p.386].

And finally, consider the first of the rules of civility George Washington lived by:

> Every action done in company ought to be done with some sign of respect to those that are present [Brookhiser, 1997, p.27].

Note the recurrence of the key concept: *respect.* As I've said, I don't think it needs further definition when presented as a code—you risk bogging down in the detail if you do. I'm reminded of a past client who was under investigation for tolerating sexual harassment in his department. He wasn't the perpetrator, but he was accused of failing to set limits on subordinates engaged in inappropriate conduct. "How the heck am I supposed to know how the company defines sexual harassment?!" An abrasive type (for reasons that will soon become obvious), he insisted it was impossible to enforce ambiguity: "When our HR person did the training, we kept drilling her on exactly what qualifies as harassment. Every time we challenged her, she kept saying that it isn't always clear-cut. By the time we were done with her, she left the room in tears." What a peach—he obviously relished his role of devil's advocate, which in turn spurred me to bedevil him with insight. I explained that he was both right and wrong. He was right about universal standards: they aren't specific enough to stipulate the correct response for every conceivable circumstance. He was wrong, though, in the belief that one could draft a standard specific enough to address *all* circumstances. That's why our legal system includes judges—it's their role to interpret the letter of the law. In the practice of law, it's their responsibility to read and interpret the meaning of a law as it applies to a given situation, much as it is the responsibility of bosses to read and interpret the behavior of employees in a given situation through the exercise of empathy. My client fled his responsibility to ensure respectful workplace conduct on the grounds that it would require him to interpret ambiguous standards into specific limits—*guilty as charged.* Don't get roped into specific definitions of disrespectful behavior—you'll only end up tied in knots. The better path is to create a general standard calling for respect and then hold bosses responsible for interpreting the spirit of the law as it applies to specific circumstances.

One other recommendation: forget the ol' Golden Rule when you're contemplating codes. The "do unto others as you would have them do unto you" approach backfires badly when applied by some abrasive bosses; they grew accustomed to poor treatment in childhood, to the point where they blindly inflict it as adults. These individuals will take the Golden Rule and do unto others as others once did unto them—and not see the harm in it. Here's another insight that may prove handy: my twist on the definition of professional conduct, custom-tailored to my abrasive clients:

> Professional conduct: Treating others with respect *whether or not you respect them*.

I can't tell you how sick I am of the statement, "People have to *earn* my respect before I'll treat them with respect"—that one really sets my teeth on edge. However, because I conduct myself professionally, I promptly retract my fangs and explain that the eye-for-an-eye approach, when used to accord respect, suggests extreme emotional *un*intelligence. If bosses balk at rendering respect until everyone else earns theirs, they're going to be waiting a long time—up to and including forever. I consider it, well, emotionally *stupid* to predicate one's behavior on the behavior of others—they can take the low road, but I'll take the high road.

Communicate the Code

Call your company's code whatever you want—Code of Interpersonal Conduct; Code of Coworker Conduct; Policy for Dignity—it makes no difference to me. But once you name it, communicate it: write it up in policy manuals and on placards, and talk it up, starting at the top of your company's dominance hierarchy and not shutting up until everyone knows about it. You can find guides or consultants who can help you with these steps, but don't take *any* steps unless you fully intend to take the third step to prevent workplace abrasion.

Live the Code

In other words *walk the talk*. Don't bother to set a standard for interpersonal conduct if you're not willing to live up to it. Don't expect "do as I say and not as I do" to do the trick here. Leaders (of families or businesses) need to set the example to convince others to "do as I say *and* as I do." Don't waste your breath declaring a dogma of dignity if you're not willing to model the concept, because actions speak louder than words. Employees may hear your words, but they'll absorb them only through organizational osmosis: it's up to you to become the behavioral pacemaker modeling the practice of respect.

Enforce the Code

When you walk the talk, walk softly, but carry a big threat—the threat of consequences for disrespectful conduct. Setting limits isn't enough: monitoring mechanisms (climate surveys, for example) designed to continuously gauge respect levels should be installed, and bosses should be held accountable for investigating incidents of interpersonal incompetence. Last but not least, employees must have safe ways of reporting breaches of the code, either through the chain of command, human resources, or a company hotline.

A Final Note

Turning a blind eye to workplace abrasion is unacceptable and unethical. Taming abrasive bosses and preventing further abrasion in the workplace will require the same techniques used to take people's blinders off and make society care enough about other forms of abuse to outlaw them. The time has come to seek solutions to this problem through continuing research and empathy-based interventions. We need to stop demonizing abrasive bosses and start treating workplace abrasion with all due respect for the problem, the perpetrators, and for the organizations that perpetuate the pain. It is my deepest hope that this boss whisperer's insights will lead to happier trails for you and those you work over, under, and with.

Appendix

Are You Abrasive?
(Self-Test)

1. Have you ever been asked to:
   a. Improve your communication skills
   b. Control your temper
   c. Learn to get along with others
   d. Not get so "worked up"
   e. Not be so hard on coworkers

2. Have you been passed over for promotion and can't get anyone to give you specific reasons for the decision?

3. Have you been passed over for promotion because of your people management skills?

4. Do you find yourself in intense and unresolved confrontations with
   a. Superiors
   b. Peers
   c. Subordinates
   d. Human resource staff

5. Have complaints been brought against you for inappropriate conduct, such as
   a. Harassment
   b. Discrimination
   c. Hostile treatment

6. Do you have a nickname that refers to dangerous behaviors (such as "Axe-Man," "Terminator," "The Ripper") or dangerous animals ("Pit Bull," "Wildebeest," "Tyrannosaurus")?

7. Do people avoid you at work?

8. Do employees attempt to transfer out of your department or avoid transferring into it?

9. Do you have enemies at work? If so, how many?

10. Do you frequently find yourself intensely frustrated by coworkers?

11. Do you generally feel that you are smarter than your coworkers?

12. Do people choose their words very carefully so as not to offend you?

13. Have you received low scores for team building, participative management, or other so-called "soft" skills on a management skills assessment?

14. Do you dislike coworkers who are less competent than you?

15. Do you take pleasure in demonstrating to others that they are less competent?

16. If so, do you openly refer to selected coworkers as
    a. Lazy
    b. Stupid
    c. Incompetent
    d. A bunch of idiots
    e. Other pejorative descriptions

17. Do you engage in any of the following behaviors at work?
    a. Publicly criticizing others
    b. Hostile humor or teasing

c. Shouting

d. Profanity

e. Making threats

f. Publicly humiliating others

g. Temper outbursts

h. Physical intimidation (such as throwing objects or slamming doors)

i. Ignoring others or giving others the silent treatment

j. Name-calling

k. Making condescending statements

l. Nonverbal expressions of disdain (rolling eyeballs, snorting, snickering, and so on)

Scoring

- If you answered yes to *any* of the following questions, there is a strong possibility that you are perceived as abrasive: 2, 3, 7, 9, 10, 11, 12, 13, 14.

- If you answered yes to *any* of the remaining questions, *you are behaving abrasively:* 1, 4, 5, 6, 8, 15, 16, 17. These questions refer to unacceptable workplace behavior or extreme coworker reactions signifying abrasion.

Recommendations

- **Get as much feedback as you can, as soon as you can.** Make it easy (in other words, nonthreatening) for others to give you feedback. Tell them you are concerned that you may be coming across in ways that you do not intend, and reassure them that you will be grateful for their frank input. Listen calmly, take notes, ask questions for clarification, and above all *do not attempt to defend yourself.* The goal is to collect data on how you are perceived, period.

- **Apologize.** "I see now that when I interrupt, it may give the impression that I think my thoughts are more valuable. I don't mean to give that impression, and I'm sorry that I did."

- **Ask for further feedback.** "If you see me doing that again, will you let me know? I'd appreciate it."

- **Thank coworkers for having the courage to open up, and reassure them that they are helping—not harming— you.** "Thanks again for speaking frankly. It really helped—it opened my eyes."

- **Get help if you are unable to change your abrasive behavior.** Ask your employer to refer you to a specialist who works with abrasive individuals, and if that's not an option, seek help on your own.

References

Babiak, P., & Hare, R. D. (2006). *Snakes in suits: When psychopaths go to work.* New York: HarperCollins, Regan Books.

Bing, S. (1992). *Crazy bosses: Spotting them, serving them, surviving them.* New York: Morrow.

Brookhiser, R. (1996). *Founding father: Rediscovering George Washington.* New York: Free Press.

Brookhiser, R. (1997). *Rules of civility: The 110 precepts that guided our first president in war and peace.* New York: Free Press.

Buck, R., & Ginsburg, B. (1997). Communicative genes and the evolution of empathy. In W. Ickes (Ed.), *Empathic accuracy* (pp. 17–43). New York: Guilford Press.

Bureau of National Affairs. (1990). *Violence and stress: The work/family connection* (Special Report No. 32). Washington, DC: Author.

Carroll, L. (1941). *Alice's adventures in Wonderland.* New York: Heritage Press. (Original work published 1865)

Cloudsley-Thompson, J. L. (1980). *Tooth and claw: Defensive strategies in the animal world.* London: Dent.

Crawshaw, L. (2005). *Coaching abrasive executives: Exploring the use of empathy in constructing less destructive interpersonal management strategies.* Unpublished doctoral dissertation, Fielding Graduate University, Santa Barbara, California.

Darwin, C. (1965). *Expression of the emotions in man and animals.* New York: Philosophical Library. (Original work published 1872)

Di Genio, J. (2002). The toxic boss. *The Armed Forces Comptroller, 47*(1), 14–19.

Felder, L. (1993). *Does someone at work treat you badly?* New York: Berkley Books.

Freud, S. (1960). *Jokes and their relation to the unconscious.* New York: Norton. (Original work published 1905)

Gibson, J. J. (1979). *The ecological approach to visual perception.* Boston: Houghton Mifflin.

Goleman, D. (1998). *Working with emotional intelligence.* New York: Bantam.

Harlow, H. F., & Suomi, S. J. (1970). The nature of love—simplified. *American Psychologist, 25*, 161–168.

Henderson-Loney, J. E. (1996). *A study of the relationship between conditions present in managers' families of origin and the behavior of managers in workplace relationships.* Unpublished doctoral dissertation, University of San Francisco.

Herzberg, F. (1968, January/February). One more time: How do you motivate employees? *Harvard Business Review*, 53–62.

Hoel, H., & Cooper, C.L.C. (2000). *Destructive conflict and bullying at work.* Manchester, UK: University of Manchester, Institute of Science and Technology.

Hoffman, M. L. (2000). *Empathy and moral development.* New York: Cambridge University Press.

Hollenhorst, P. (1998). What do we know about anger management programs in corrections? *Federal Probation, 62*(2), 52–64.

Hornstein, H. A. (1996). *Brutal bosses and their prey: How to identify and overcome abuse in the workplace.* New York: Riverhead Books.

Ickes, W. (Ed.). (1997). *Empathic accuracy.* New York: Guilford Press.

Laabs, J. (1999). Employee sabotage: Don't be a target! *Workforce, 78*(7), 32–43.

Leary, M. R., Springer, C., Negel, L., Ansell, E., & Evans, K. (1998). The causes, phenomenology, and consequences of hurt feelings. *Journal of Personality and Social Psychology, 74*(5), 1225–1237.

Leymann, H. (1990). Mobbing and psychological terror at workplaces. *Violence and Victims, 5*(2), 119–126.

Lloyd, K. (1999). *Jerks at work.* Franklin Lakes, NJ: Career Press.

Lombardo, M. M., & McCall, M. W., Jr. (1984). *Coping with an intolerable boss* (Special Report). Greensboro, NC: Center for Creative Leadership.

Marais, S., & Herman, M. (1997). *Corporate hyenas at work: How to spot and outwit them by being hyenawise.* Pretoria: Kagiso.

Mazur, A. (2005). *Biosociology of dominance and deference.* Lanham, MD: Rowman & Littlefield.

McCarthy, P., Sheehan, M. J., & Kearns, D. (1995). *Managerial styles and their effects on employees' health and well-being in organisations undergoing restructuring* (Report for Worksafe Australia). Brisbane, Australia: Griffith University.

McLaughlin, J. (2000). Anger within. *OHS Canada, 16*(8), 30–36.

Metts, S. (1994). Relational transgressions. In W. R. Cupach & B. H. Spitzberg (Eds.), *The dark side of interpersonal communication* (pp. 217–239). Mahwah, NJ: Erlbaum.

Miller, A. (1983). *For your own good: Hidden cruelty in child-rearing and the roots of violence.* New York: Farrar, Straus & Giroux.

Miller, R. S. (2001). Breaches of propriety. In R. M. Kowalski (Ed.), *Behaving badly: Aversive behaviors in interpersonal relationships* (pp. 29–58). Washington, DC: American Psychological Association.

Namie, G., & Namie, R. (2003). *The bully at work.* Naperville, IL: Sourcebooks.

Quine, L. (1999). Workplace bullying in the NHS Community Trust: Staff questionnaire survey. *British Medical Journal, 318,* 228–232.

Rayner, C. (1997). Incidence of workplace bullying. *Journal of Community and Applied Social Psychology, 7*(3), 199–208.

Rayner, C., & Cooper, C. L. (2003). The black hole in "bullying at work" research. *International Journal of Management and Decision Making, 4*(1), 47–64.

Reed, S. F. (1993). *The toxic executive.* New York: HarperCollins.

Richman, J. A., Rospenda, K. M., Flaherty, J. A., & Freels, S. (2001). Workplace harassment, active coping, and alcohol-related outcomes. *Journal of Substance Abuse, 13*(3), 347–366.

Smith, R. N. (1994). The surprising George Washington: Part 3. *Prologue, 26*(1), 7–15.

Spherion Corporation. (1999). *Report on the Emerging Workforce Study* (Conducted in conjunction with Louis Harris & Associates, Inc.). Fort Lauderdale, FL: Author.

Sutton, R. (2007). *The no asshole rule: Building a civilized workplace and surviving one that isn't.* New York: Warner Business Books.

Whalen, P. J., Kagan, J., Cook, R. G., Davis, F. C., Kim, H., Polis, S., et al. (2004). Human amygdala responsivity to masked fearful eye whites. *Science, 306,* 2061.

Wikipedia. (2006). Definition of respect. Retrieved December 3, 2006, from http://en.wikipedia.org/wiki/Respect.

Williams, O. F. (2000). *Global codes of conduct: An idea whose time has come.* Notre Dame, IN: University of Notre Dame Press.

Work & Family Connection. (2005). *The Most Important Work-Life-Related Studies.* Minnetonka, MN: Author.

Index